MEASURING UP
on the
NEW JERSEY

H S P A

Early Preparation in Language Arts Literacy

Developed Specifically for the New Jersey HSPA

This book was designed to help you prepare to do your best
on the **New Jersey Proficiency Assessment** test given in Grade Ten.
The content, skills, and questioning techniques match the ***New Jersey Core
Curriculum Content Standards***. Instructional worktexts are available in the
content areas of language arts literacy, science,
and mathematics, and on other grade levels.
You should not wait until only a month before test time
to start preparing with this book—you should be preparing
throughout the school year.

*This book will help you develop the skills and confidence
you need to do your very best!*

The Peoples Publishing Group, Inc.

*A New Jersey Publisher Serving the Needs of
New Jersey Educators and Students*

1-800-822-1080

Editor: **BBE Associates, Ltd.**
Pre-Press & Production Manager: **Doreen Smith**
Copy Editor: **Pedra J. Del Vechio**
Production/Electronic Design: **Erika Hillefeld/Jennifer Wilhelmy**
Cover Design: **Jeremy Mayes**
Photo Research: **Kristine Liebman**

Illustrations:
Armando Baéz
Eric Grajo
Erika Hillefeld

Photo Credits:
Archive Photos
Hebgen Lake Ranger District, West Yellowstone, Montana
National Aeronautics and Space Administration (NASA)

ISBN 1-56256-273-8

Copyright © 2000
The Peoples Publishing Group, Inc.
299 Market Street
Saddle Brook, New Jersey 07663

Printed in the United States of America.

10   9   8   7   6   5   4   3

❖ Table of Contents ❖

Classroom
Discussion

How do you find topics to write or speak on that are interesting? Why is it easier to create a report or speech on a topic that interests you? How do you form opinions about a topic? How can research change your opinions?

Classroom
Activity

Look at the picture below. Answer the questions that follow.

1. What topic does this photograph suggest to you?

_____

_____

_____

_____

2. What details do you notice in this photograph?

_____

_____

_____

_____

3. What do the details add to the topic?

_____

_____

_____

_____

4. What conclusion can you draw by studying this photograph?

_____

_____

_____

_____

5. Would this photograph make a better topic for a speech or a written report? Why?

_____

_____

_____

_____

Language Arts

Prewriting: Setting Purpose
(Entertain, Inform, Persuade, and Instruct)

Classroom Discussion

How would people react if the President of the United States told jokes all through an important speech on foreign policy? What if a TV comedy show tried to teach its audience how to do car repairs? How does the purpose of a presentation affect its style and content?

Classroom Activity

Read the following information. Then answer the questions in the boxes.

Before you write a report or prepare a speech, **set a purpose** for your work. Your purpose is how you want to affect your audience. Why are they reading what you have written? Why are they listening to you speak? The four main purposes for writing or speaking are:

- **Entertain**–to make your audience laugh, cry, shiver with fright, or thrill with suspense.
- **Inform**–to present facts about real people, places, events, or ideas.
- **Persuade**–to convince your audience to believe or do something.
- **Instruct or give directions**–to teach your audience how something is done.

By first setting a purpose, you can focus on what the main points of your presentation should be. Details that don't contribute to your purpose can be left out.

At a televised meeting of the City Council, you're going to make a short speech. Donations are needed for a special fund. The fund will be used to send doctors and medicines to help children in Central America. How do you define the purpose of your speech?

Step 1

Decide on the purpose for your speech.

1. **What will you be talking about in your speech?**

_____

_____

2. **How do you want your audience to react to your speech?**

_____

_____

3. **Which of the four purposes outlined above fits your speech?**

_____

_____

Step 2

Identify the audience for your speech.

4. Who will be listening to your speech?

_____

_____

_____

5. What will your audience want to get from your speech?

_____

_____

_____

_____

Step 3

Decide how to prepare your speech so that you will achieve your purpose.

6. Should your speech be in a style that is casual or formal? Why? (Think of your audience.)

_____

_____

7. What facts should you include in your speech?

_____

_____

_____

8. Read the following opening sentences. Which would be best for your speech? Circle the letter of your answer.

   a. The countries that make up Central America are Guatemala, Belize, El Salvador, Honduras, Nicaragua, Costa Rica, and Panama.

   b. Doctors may be highly educated but they're as absent-minded as the rest of us when packing for a trip to another country.

   c. Small donations for medicines and doctor's visits can make a big difference to the health of children living in Central America.

   d. To set up a medical mission to Central America, you first must contact the authorities in each country and discuss your plans.

 Language Arts

Open-Ended Question

9. Think about your answer to this question. Write your answer on the lines. Be prepared to talk about your answer in a classroom discussion. If you were hired by the Red Cross to write a 10-second radio commercial to get donations, what would you say in the commercial?

_____

_____

_____

_____

_____

_____

_____

Ideas to Remember

set a purpose–decide on the reason for your writing or speech

entertain–present material so that an audience laughs, or feels sad, frightened, or thrilled

inform–present facts about real people, places, events, or ideas

persuade–convince an audience to believe or do something

instruct–teach an audience how something is done

Guided Practice Activity

You've been chosen to deliver a report to an American History class about the Negro Leagues. These were the early baseball leagues in which African Americans played. After the report, you'll lead a question-and-answer session. Read the paragraphs below. Then answer the questions.

A. The feats of some Negro League stars were legendary. Josh Gibson, known as "the black Babe Ruth," was the greatest home run hitter of his time. One day, he hit a tremendous shot over the center field fence to win a game in Cleveland. During the next day's game in Pittsburgh, a ball suddenly dropped out of the sky. The center fielder for the other team caught the ball. "You're out!"roared the umpire, looking at Josh. "Yesterday—in Cleveland!"

B. Since the 1890s, African Americans had been barred from playing alongside white players in the major leagues. Teams of black players were forced into semipro leagues or barnstorming tours. Then in 1920 an African American named Andrew "Rube" Foster had a great idea. Foster had been a star player years before, and he knew a lot about baseball. He gathered the owners of the most successful African American teams in the country. They met in Kansas City to discuss his plan for a new league. It became the Negro National League.

GO TO NEXT PAGE

C. To find out more about the Negro Leagues, the library is the best place to start. A good introduction to the subject is a book called *Only the Ball Was White* by Robert Peterson, a respected historian. Another excellent book, filled with photographs of the greatest African American players, is *The Negro Leagues* by David Craft. On video, look for Ken Burns' documentary called *Baseball*. Burns tells the story of the Negro Leagues and the breaking of the color line in major league baseball. You might also watch the video movie *Bingo Long and his Traveling All-Stars*. It is a fictionalized version of a barnstorming black baseball team. And don't forget to visit the Negro Leagues Baseball Museum in Kansas City.

D. There should be more of the early African American stars in baseball's Hall of Fame. One can read story after story of how well these players did in exhibition games against major leaguers. Satchel Paige used to strike out more than ten major league stars in each game. Rube Foster taught his screwball pitch to the white pitchers on the New York Giants, which helped the Giants win the National League. An African American catcher named Bruce Petway threw out the speedy Ty Cobb twice in one game. And if "Cool Papa" Bell had played in the white major leagues, he would have challenged Cobb's base-stealing records.

Step 1

Decide on the purpose for your report.

10. What will you be talking about in your report?

_____

11. How do you want your audience to react to your report?

_____

_____

12. Which of the four purposes outlined above fits your speech?

_____

Step 2

Identify the audience for your speech.

13. Who will be listening to your speech?

_____

14. What will your audience want to get from your report?

_____

_____

Step 3

Decide how to prepare your report so that you will achieve your purpose.

15. Should your report be in a style that is casual or formal? Why?

_____

16. What facts should you include in your speech?

_____

_____

17. Which of the paragraphs above would make a good opening paragraph for your report? Why?

_____

_____

_____

18. If you were invited back to the American History class to deliver a more casual, entertaining talk about the Negro Leagues, which paragraph above would you include? Why?

_____

_____

Application Activity

Read each paragraph. Identify the purpose of each paragraph and write it on the line. Then answer the questions that follow.

19. The rain refused to stop, my parents were still out shopping, and I still had my 4-year-old brother Kip to babysit. So, genius that I am, I decided to teach Kip how to play chess. While removing the pieces from the box, he became infatuated with his knights, which he called "horseys." Slowly, one by one, the pieces found their proper squares—although not before Kip had examined each one closely and sucked on a pawn or two. Now came the hard part: explaining how the pieces moved. I went through all the possibilities very carefully, and was pleased to see Kip paying such close attention. "Now," I said, testing his knowledge, "how does a knight move?" Kip picked up the piece, looked it in the eye, placed it on the board, and began jumping it around the squares in a sort of leaping gallop. The other pieces stood stock still, hoping to avoid this runaway horse on their battleground.

_____

20. To play chess, you must first place the pieces correctly on the board. Each player employs a set of 16 "chessmen." One set is light-colored and is called "white." The other set is dark-colored and is called "black." Each player's set has eight pawns. The other eight chessmen in a set are called pieces. The pieces include, in order of rank, a king, a queen, two rooks, two bishops, and two knights. Before you start the game, arrange your pieces on the row of the chessboard that is nearest to you. Place the rooks in the corner squares. Next to them go the knights and then the bishops. Place the queen in the central square of its own color, light or dark. Your king stands next to the queen and faces the opposing king directly across the board. Place your row of pawns in front of the row of pieces.

21. Chess pieces have been made in many different patterns, from simple to beautifully fancy. Some early European chess pieces were made from gold or silver and included jewels and enamel surfaces. The queens and kings were dressed in royal clothing. The knights wore armor and the pawns carried spears or looked like foot soldiers. Chess pieces from India or the Middle East were also ornate. The rooks were carved elephants and the knights rode camels instead of horses. The Chinese designed pieces to look like warriors, although some preferred simple pieces that looked more like checkers. As chess became widely popular, a simple standard design was created by Howard Staunton in 1849. However, some fancy chess sets were still produced. For example, one famous set was made up of characters from Shakespeare's *Macbeth*.

22. Which would be the best audience for the paragraph in 19?

a. members of the Chess Club meeting to discuss membership dues

b. readers of a newspaper section called "Kids Will Be Kids," which uses contributions from readers

c. users of an Internet site called StrategicChess.com

d. readers of a Russian chess magazine called *8 x 8*

23. Which would be the best audience for the paragraph in 20?

a. a group of older children at the city park wanting to learn new games

b. a group of longtime chess players in the park

c. users of an Internet site called StrategicChess.com

d. a group of junior high students who enjoy playing video games

24. Write down what group would be a good audience for the paragraph in 21.

Language Arts

Open-Ended
Question

25. Use a separate piece of paper or write in your literary response journal. Refer to the information in this lesson. Chess is a very old game. What games that are played now will still be played 500 years in the future?

Extension Activities

Reading Prompt ● The Purpose of Newspaper Articles and Features

Individual Activity

26. **Go through today's newspaper and look at the various articles and features. Decide on the purpose of each and label it. Some articles and features may have more than one purpose. Compile your findings into a chart. In the last column of the chart, describe the audience for each article or feature. Which purpose appears most frequently in your chart? Which is least frequent?**

_____

_____

_____

_____

Speaking Prompt ● Comparing Literary Treatments of a Subject

Cooperative Group Activity

27. **Work with a partner. Look through the local television listings or the current issue of _TV Guide_. Find five programs that are intended to entertain. Then find five programs for each of the other three categories: inform, persuade, and instruct. Watch one of the programs in each category. Discuss the programs you watched with your partner. For each one, write a paragraph on a separate sheet of paper describing what the program was about and how well it accomplished its purpose.**

_____

_____

_____

Speaking Prompt ● Discuss Ethical Problems Related to Technology Use

Workplace Readiness Activity

28. **Work with a group. Hold a discussion about advertising on the Internet and how it is done. Should any site be able to include advertising? Should the kind of advertising that is allowed depend on the purpose of the site where it appears? Should some products not be advertised on the Internet because the ads might be seen by children? How can the types and amount of advertising on the Internet be controlled without interfering with freedom of speech? Encourage each member of the group to express his or her opinions.**

_____

_____

_____

Classroom Discussion

If you are going to write a report or speech, how do you decide what to write about? How do you know what to research and include in your report?

Classroom Activity

Read and examine the information below. Answer the questions that follow.

The first step to writing a report or speech is to determine a topic. If your topic is too broad, your writing will have no focus. If your topic is too narrow, you will not find enough information to write about.

After you decide on a topic, you must then do research. As you are researching, you must determine K—what you already **know** about the topic, W—what you **want** to know about the topic, and L—what you have **learned** from doing your research.

Your assignment is to write a report about the Dust Bowl in the western part of the United States during the 1930s. The following information can be used to determine a topic for your paper and to determine what you know, what you want to know, and what you have learned.

In the late 1920s and early 1930s, farming practices were building up to help nature create one of the greatest tragedies in United States history. Farmers in the central part of the Great Plains plowed away the thick prairie grass that had grown for centuries and replaced it with wheat. The fertile land grew so much wheat that people from all over the country moved to the Plains to become wheat farmers. Wheat was making the farming community wealthy. However, growing wheat and no other crop was taking all the minerals out of the soil so that eventually nothing grew well. Trees had been cut in order to clear fields for planting. This meant that little vegetation remained to hold the soil in place, and erosion was a constant danger. Also, the plows that had cut into the prairie to prepare the soil for planting had only scratched the surface of the land and left a thick layer of powdery dust on the top of the earth. All of these problems combined with a drought and high winds to create what has become known as the "Dust Bowl."

The land became dry, and no crops would grow, and so the soil was left open to erosion. Drought left the soil dry, and plowing had left it like powder. When the hot winds began to blow, they picked up the dry, dusty powder and carried it away. Winds that blew from the south and west threw the dust high into the air and scattered it like a thin veil of dirt. Winds that blew from the north kept the dust clouds close to the ground so that dust and dirt billowed across the land, choking people and animals. Farmers could not grow crops, and to save themselves from starvation, they packed up and left their farms. People who stayed watched the wind carry their once fertile topsoil to other parts of the country. Banks reclaimed farms that had been abandoned, but they could do little with the land because it could not be farmed. The futures of many banks were threatened because they had invested money in assets that could not be resold.

  Language Arts

Step 1

Decide on your topic.

1. **What is the topic of these paragraphs?**

   _____

2. **Why could you not use the topic "The Dust Bowl"?**

   _____

3. **Could you use the topic "The Effects of Southern Wind"? Why?**

   _____

Step 2

As you read, determine what information you already **know** about your topic.

4. **What kinds of information might already be familiar to you?**

   _____

   _____

   _____

Step 3

As you read, determine what information you **want** to know for your report.

5. **If you were writing a report about the causes of the Dust Bowl, what kinds of information from these paragraphs would you want to know?**

   _____

   _____

   _____

Step 4

As you read, determine what new information you have **learned**.

6. **What new information have you learned about this period of American history?**

   _____

   _____

   _____

   _____

Open-Ended Question

7. Think about your answer to the following question. Write your answer on the lines. Be prepared to talk about your answer in a classroom discussion. Using what information you may have about farming, or what you know about growing plants, how have our farming methods changed to ensure that another Dust Bowl does not happen?

_____

_____

_____

_____

_____

_____

Ideas to Remember

> **topic**–the person, place, thing, or idea that a writer or speaker is discussing
>
> **KWL**–what a reader **knows** about a chosen topic, what a reader **wants** to know about the topic, and what the reader has **learned** while reading about the topic

Guided Practice Activity

Read the following information and answer the questions in the boxes.

One of the most important duties of George Washington as our first President was to set behavior standards for whoever holds the office of President. When Washington was elected, people did not even know what to call him. A Senate committee who had been assigned the task of coming up with a title for the newly elected officer suggested, "His Highness the President of the United States and Protector of the Rights of the Same." After having fought a war to be free of the English King George, Washington felt that the last thing people in the United States would want would be another king. Washington, however, feared to become too familiar with the people around him for fear that people would not respect the office. Alexander Hamilton dared one of Washington's close friends to pat him on the shoulder at a gathering. At the gathering, Gouverneur Morris, Washington's friend, walked up to Washington and patted him on the shoulder. Saying nothing, Washington coldly stared at Morris until Morris withdrew his hand and disappeared into the crowd. Think about our modern presidents. Are people allowed to approach and touch them whenever they want?

Washington liked to meet with people who could inform him of how his government was accepted among the people. He held gatherings at least once a week. One of his aides decided the gatherings required more formality, and he flung open the door to the room where Washington was standing and announced in a loud voice, "The Pres-i-dent of the U-ni-ted States!" Washington was terribly embarrassed. After the gathering he informed the man that the incident would never happen again. Afterwards, Washington waited in the reception room, and the crowd of guests entered to greet him.

GO TO NEXT PAGE

 Language Arts

Step 1

Decide on your topic.

8. **What is the topic of the report?**

_____

_____

Step 2

As you read, determine what information you already **know** about your topic.

9. **What information did you already know about the topic?**

_____

_____

Step 3

As you read, determine what information you **want** to know for your report.

10. **What information would you want to know for a report on Washington as the first president?**

_____

_____

Step 4

As you read, determine what new information you have **learned**.

11. **What information did you learn from reading these two paragraphs that you did not know before?**

_____

_____

_____

_____

_____

13

Application Activity

Imagine that you are going to write a report on cash registers. Read the following paragraphs. As you read, think about what information you knew already, what information you would need to know for your report, and what new information you learned while reading.

The National Cash Register Company was built in Dayton, Ohio, by a man named John H. Patterson. At the age of twenty-five, Patterson had started his first business as a coal dealer. He acquired coal from companies that mined it and sold it to customers. He expanded his businesses to include ownership in a coal mine, in a railroad, and in a retail store that sold mining supplies. The only business that lost money was his store. After months of work, Patterson found out why the losses in the store occurred. Clerks were not only making mistakes as they gave people their change, they were stealing from the money drawer. Not only were the clerks guilty, but the bookkeepers who kept track of the money made mistakes, either honestly or on purpose. Patterson put a stop to the loss of money when he bought two mechanical cashiers from their inventor, James Ritty. Ritty was not a businessman, and his company soon was in danger of bankruptcy. Patterson decided that the reason for Ritty's failure was that not enough people knew about his machines.

After buying the company, Patterson tried to sell it back to Ritty when he found out how the company had been run and what its property was like. Ritty refused to buy back the failing company, and Patterson began a campaign to build a successful company. He began by using a direct mail approach to merchants. He badgered people until some of them agreed to buy his machines. He then hired sales people and guaranteed them a territory and commission. He taught his sales force how to be polite to customers and how to convince them to buy. He held yearly sales conventions to praise successful sales people and to fire those whose sales were not high.

Patterson next concentrated on production. He moved his office to the assembly area. He found that the workers were dissatisfied and that they sent out damaged equipment to get even with the company. Patterson rebuilt the factory and included walls of windows so that the workers could get light and fresh air. Then he established several programs to help them, including company-provided lunches in a cafeteria, safety shields to protect people from dangerous equipment, parks for the employees' enjoyment, and dressing rooms and showers to be used on company time. Patterson even built a gym and required that all employees exercise at some time during each day in order to feel healthier, and thus happier. He also set up night classes to educate his factory workers. Patterson's goal was to increase sales and production by making his workers happy.

12. What information did you find in these paragraphs that you already knew about cash registers?

_____

13. What information do you feel you would need to know in order to write a report about cash registers?

_____

14. What information have you just learned to help you write a complete report about cash registers?

_____

 Language Arts

Open-Ended Question

15. Use a separate piece of paper or write in your literary response journal. Refer to the information in the Application Activity.

- How could sales conventions help the sales force of a company?

- How could improvements that Patterson made in the factory help to improve the amount of production?

Extension Activities

Speaking Prompt ● Examining Information

16. **Explain in a short speech to the group why it is important to determine what information you already know about a topic as opposed to what information you will need to know in order to write a report.**

_____

_____

Individual Activity

Reading Prompt ● Identifying Material for Reports

17. **Work with a group. Have each member of the group identify reports that they will have to complete soon. Ask each member to select a topic for that report and write information they already know about it. Then have each member determine what kind of information they will still need in order to complete the report.**

_____

_____

_____

_____

Cooperative Group Activity

Speaking Prompt ● Using Critical Thinking Skills

18. **Work with a group. Brainstorm practices that you feel would be helpful to employees on assembly lines and practices that would improve employee morale. Think back on some of the provisions that John Patterson made for his workers. Design a work area for assembly line workers, and describe company practices that would help keep employees happy and productive. Present your design and descriptions in a speech before the class.**

_____

_____

_____

Workplace Readiness Activity

Lesson 1C

Prewriting: Taking Notes
(Including Sources and Avoiding Plagiarism)

Classroom
Discussion

If someone recommends a movie to see, how do you make note of it so you'll remember? Why is it helpful to take notes on the books and articles you read? How do you organize notes so you can use them later?

Classroom
Activity

Read the following information. Then answer the questions in the boxes.

Once you've selected a topic, you must begin looking for information about that topic. This will add to your knowledge. Since you can't remember everything you read, you need to **take notes** on the material you find. The best notes provide two kinds of information:

- the most important details about your topic.

- the source of the information, or where it came from.

Learn to take notes only on the topic that you're researching. If your topic is "How the United States Entered World War II," your notes shouldn't include information about how World War II ended. Also, put your notes in outline form. This makes it easy to separate the most important points from the minor details.

Include the **source** for every piece of information you find, even the ones you may not use. You might decide later to use them and then you'll need the source. For each source, write the title, the author, the publisher (or, for articles, the name of the magazine or newspaper), and the date the material appeared. Be careful to avoid **plagiarism**, or the unlawful copying of material that is under copyright. Always **paraphrase** the information you find. That means rewriting it in your own words. If the ideas or information you use is not common knowledge, you must also cite the sources for this material. When in doubt, always cite your sources in detail.

Your assignment is to write about Shirley Temple's career as a child actress in motion pictures. In your research, you locate the following information.

Shirley Temple was the most famous child actress in movie history. Her dimples, curly hair, beaming smile, and dancing feet made her the favorite of audiences in the 1930s. She was born Shirley Jane Temple on April 23, 1928, in Santa Monica, California. Her first feature-film appearance came in 1932. For the next 10 years she made one popular movie after another. One of the best was *Bright Eyes*, in which she sang "On the Good Ship Lollipop." From 1935 to 1938, she was the number one box office draw in Hollywood. At her peak, she earned $100,000 per film—quite a tidy sum for the 1930s!

After her movie career ended, Shirley continued to be successful. In 1950 she married Charles A. Black and had two children. In the 1960s she became U.S. ambassador to Ghana, and then the protocol chief for the entire Foreign Service. She was the first woman to ever hold the latter job.

—from *Shirley Temple, the Dimpled Darling* by Elsa Wallach, Zenith Books, 1985.

GO TO NEXT PAGE

Language Arts

Lesson 1c

Step 1

Take notes on the most important details relating to your topic.

1. **What is the topic of the first paragraph?**
   _____

2. **What is the topic of the second paragraph?**
   _____

3. **Which paragraph has information that would be helpful in writing your report?**
   _____

4. **What details would you write in your notes?**
   _____
   _____
   _____
   _____
   _____
   _____

Step 2

Write your notes in outline form.

I. **Shirley Temple**
   A. **The most famous child actress in movie history**
      1. **born Shirley Jane Temple on April 23, 1928, in Santa Monica, California**
      2. **dimples, curly hair, beaming smile, and dancing feet**
   B. **Movie Career**
      1. **first feature film appearance in 1932**
      2. **made popular movies for 10 years**
      3. **was number-one box office draw from 1935 to 1938**
      4. **at her peak, she earned $100,000 per film—quite a sum for a little princess of the 1930s!**

5. **How would this outline help you write a report on your topic?**
   _____

6. **What is plagiarism?**
   _____

7. **What note should be paraphrased to avoid plagiarism?**
   _____

8. **Rewrite that note here.**
   _____

Step 3

Identify your source for the information.

9. **What is a source?**

_____

10. **What is the source for this information about Shirley Temple?**

_____

11. **What kind of source is it?**

_____

Open-Ended Question

12. Think about your answer to this question. Write your answer on the lines. Be prepared to talk about your answer in a classroom discussion. Why do you think audiences in the Great Depression of the 1930s enjoyed movies so much?

_____

_____

_____

_____

_____

Ideas to Remember

taking notes–a skill that combines gathering important details about a topic and noting the source of the information

source–the place (such as a book, magazine, or newspaper) where information is obtained

plagiarism–unlawful copying of material that is under copyright

paraphrase–rewriting material in your own words

Guided Practice Activity

You are assigned to write a report on Robert Frost's career as a poet and teacher. In your research you locate the two paragraphs below. Read the paragraphs. Then answer the questions in the boxes.

The life of the poet Robert Frost was filled with contradictions. Most of his life he was connected with the farm country of the Northeast, yet he was born in California. Few poets are more closely identified with their own country than Frost, the rugged American. Yet Frost's first books of poetry were published in England. Frost wrote mainly about country life and ordinary people, yet his books appeal to all kinds of readers the world over.

GO TO NEXT PAGE

 Language Arts

Frost also had a career as a teacher of sorts. He never graduated from college, yet he taught and won honors at Harvard, Michigan, and other great universities. As a teacher, he had no set program. Instead of lecturing his students, he would chat with them. He encouraged them to think creatively. His best accomplishment was to get young people excited about language and poetry.

—from "Another Look at Frost," by John Manningham
in the *Vanguard Review*, April-May, 1992.

Step 1

Take notes on the most important details relating to your topic.

13. What is the topic of the first paragraph?

_____

14. What is the topic of the second paragraph?

_____

15. Which paragraph has information that would be helpful in writing your report?

_____

16. What details would you write in your notes?

_____

_____

_____

_____

_____

_____

_____

Step 2

Write your notes in outline form.

17. Complete the following outline.

   I. The poet Robert Frost

   A. Life filled with contradictions

   1. _____

   2. **few poets are more closely identified with their own country than Frost, the rugged American, yet Frost's first books of poetry were published in England**

   3. _____

   B. Frost the teacher

   1. _____

   2. _____

   3. _____

GO TO NEXT PAGE

18. Rewrite note I.A.2. above to avoid plagiarism.

_____

_____

_____

_____

Step 3

Identify your
source for the
information.

19. What is the source for this information about Robert Frost?

_____

_____

20. What kind of source is it?

_____

Application Activity

You're writing a report on female stars in pop music. Read the paragraphs. On your own paper, take notes on the important points. Then write your notes in the outline form below. Be sure to write your notes in your own words.

Alanis Morissette has opened lots of doors, not only for herself but for other female singers. Her 1995 album _Jagged Little Pill_, her first major-label release, has sold more than 16 million copies in the U.S. alone. Record companies learned that there was a huge audience for young girls singing songs about real life. Morissette's songs, such as "Hand in My Pocket," "Ironic," and "You Learn," connected with an audience that saw their own lives reflected in the words. The album went on to win four Grammy awards. Videos of her hit songs won heavy airplay on MTV. And suddenly record companies were searching for more young female singers. Some of their finds included Natalie Imbruglia, Lauryn Hill, and Jewel.

But for Alanis, all that success was almost too much too soon. The native of Ottawa, Canada, took a year and a half off and even considered ending her career. She needed to figure out what was most important to her. She bought a house in Los Angeles and took life easy for awhile. Soon her ideas started flowing again. The result, in 1998, was her second album, _Supposed Former Infatuation Junkie_. Once again Alanis came up with a great mixture of rockers and ballads with words that didn't settle for old pop-song cliches. Her fans were thrilled to see Alanis back on tour, singing the songs they love. Perhaps some future star will hear her and be inspired to record her own great album.

GO TO NEXT PAGE

21. Create an outline of the paragraphs.

I. General Topic: _____

   A. _____

      1. _____

      2. _____

         _____

      3. _____

         _____

      4. Record companies found other young female singers

         a. _____

         b. _____

         c. _____

   B. Alanis's success was almost too much, too soon

      1. _____

      2. _____

      3. _____

         _____

      4. _____

      5. _____

**Open-Ended
Question**

22. Use a separate piece of paper or write in your literary response journal. Refer to the information in this lesson. How does the success of one artist, singer, or performer help other, similar performers have a chance to be successful?

Lesson *1c*

Extension Activities

Writing Prompt ● Compiling Notes about Movie Reviews

Individual Activity

23. Choose a major new movie release and look up five different reviews of the film. For each review, take notes about the important points the reviewer makes. Does the reviewer like the film? Why or why not? What does the reviewer think about the story, the acting, the music, and the camera work? Carefully note the source of each review that you read, including the name of the publication, the date, and the name of the reviewer. Compile your notes into a short article about how the movie has been reviewed. What is the main topic of your article? Have the reviews been mostly favorable or unfavorable? Make sure you don't plagiarize any sentences from the reviewers. Show your article to a group of other students or e-mail it to several friends.

Reading Prompt ● Taking Notes about a Current News Story

Cooperative Group Activity

24. Work with a partner or small group. Choose a current news story that is featured on news reports or in the newspaper for several days running. Take turns taking notes on the new details of the story that come out each day. Write down the source of your notes, and look in the library or on the Internet for other sources of information about this topic. Use your notes to create an outline. Discuss how you could use the outline to write a report about this story and how it was covered on television and in the newspaper.

Speaking Prompt ● Set Short-Term and Long-Term Goals

Workplace Readiness Activity

25. Work with a group. Discuss the importance of setting short-term and long-term goals when planning a career. Talk about various careers and what goals you might set to be successful in those fields. Divide into smaller groups. Come up with a list of four or five careers and choose one to study in detail. Look in books and magazines to find information about the academic skills and the practical experience needed for that career. Make notes on the information you find and the sources. With your group, make a list of appropriate short-term and long-term goals for the career you chose. Use your notes to help you define these goals. Make a report on your findings to the larger group. Discuss how meeting those goals would help ensure a certain level of success in the field you chose.

Prewriting: Development of Central Idea and Supporting Details

Classroom Discussion

What kinds of books have you read and movies have you seen lately? What was the main point of some of these materials? What did you learn about the characters?

Classroom Activity

Read and examine the information below. Answer the questions that follow.

All writing and speeches contain **central ideas**, or the main point a writer or speaker wishes to make about a topic. These central ideas are explained and described by **supporting details**.

Plastics are probably the most commonly used substances in the world today. The vast majority of goods manufactured and sold involves the use of plastic. In the same way that iron, copper, and tin are all metals, plastics can take many forms.

There are four basic types of plastics. Some are made with cellulose, or the woody fibers from plants. Others are made from resins that occur naturally. Then there are the synthetic resins created through chemical processes. Proteins are the basis for the last group of plastics. These proteins are obtained from such things as soybeans and milk. These substances are also part of a healthy diet.

Step 1

Locate the topic of the material.

1. **Who or what is the topic of these paragraphs?**

_____

Step 2

List a few supporting details that explain the topic.

2. **How are plastics used?**

_____

3. **How many types of plastics are made?**

_____

4. **What substances are used to produce plastics?**

_____

Step 3

Create a sentence that contains these details and states the central idea of the paragraphs.

5. **Which sentence best states the central idea described by this paragraph? Circle the letter of your answer.**

a. Without plastics life would be very different for people living in the modern world.

b. Modern businesses and industry could not function without the use of plastics.

c. Four main types of plastics are used to make the vast majority of goods that are sold and used today.

Step 4

As you create written materials or speeches, be sure to avoid details that do not support the central idea.

6. **One sentence does not add more information about the four main types of plastics. It should be removed from this paragraph. Which sentence should be removed?**

_____

Open-Ended Question

7. **Think about your answer to the following question. Write your answer on the lines. Be prepared to talk about your answer in a classroom discussion. What other substances are used with and without plastics to make items that you use every day?**

_____

_____

_____

_____

_____

Ideas to Remember

> **topic**–the person, place, thing, or idea that a writer or speaker is discussing
>
> **central idea**–the most important idea about a topic
>
> **detail**–a fact or idea that tells more about a topic and the central idea about that topic
>
> **unnecessary detail**–a detail that should be removed because it does not add to the central idea

Guided Practice Activity

Read and examine the information below. Answer the questions that follow.

Before the invention of plastics, most goods were made from natural substances, such as wood, wool, cotton, iron, silver, and animal products. Ivory was an important resource in the 1800s. Buttons, piano keys, and billiard balls were only some of the products made from this resource obtained from the tusks of elephants. Years of hunting had reduced the numbers of elephants large enough to produce tusks, so ivory became rare and very expensive. Today the numbers of elephants have been so reduced that they are an endangered species. Billiard manufacturers offered a $10,000 prize for a material that could replace ivory.

GO TO NEXT PAGE

    Language Arts

Lesson 1D

Prewriting: Development of Central Idea and Supporting Details

John Wesley and Isaiah Hyatt conducted research in the United States in the hopes of winning this prize. They processed cotton to obtain cellulose, which they softened with nitric acid. Then they added camphor which turned the substance into a solid. This new substance could be formed into all types of goods. Since it was not suitable for billiard balls, the Hyatts did not win the cash prize. However, they had invented the first form of plastic—celluloid.

Step 1

Locate the topic of the material.

8. **Who or what is the topic of these paragraphs?**

_____

Step 2

List a few supporting details that explain the topic.

9. **Why did people begin carrying out experiments to find something to replace ivory?**

_____

_____

10. **How did the Hyatts produce celluloid, the first form of plastic?**

_____

_____

11. **Why were the Hyatts successful even though they had not won the prize?**

_____

_____

Step 3

Create a sentence that contains these details and states the central idea of the paragraphs.

12. **Which sentence best states the central idea described by these paragraphs? Circle the letter of your answer.**

   a. Overuse of the earth's natural resources often leads to the depletion of these resources.

   b. While experimenting to find a replacement for ivory, the Hyatt brothers of the United States invented celluloid, the first plastic.

   c. Individuals conducting research in private led to the invention of plastics and many other useful ideas.

Step 4

As you create written materials or speeches, be sure to avoid details that do not support the central idea.

13. **One sentence does not add more information about the invention of plastic. It should be removed from this paragraph. Which sentence should be removed?**

_____

Composing for Writing and Speaking

© 2000 The Peoples Publishing Group, Inc. 1-800-822-1080 **Copying Prohibited.**

Application Activity

Read the paragraphs below. Answer the questions that follow.

Celluloid soon replaced ivory as the substance turned into buttons, combs, piano keys, and eyeglass frames. Celluloid burns easily, so chemists carried out more experiments and discovered that acetic acid could be used in place of nitric acid in the Hyatts' process. The new form of celluloid is used for photographic film, safety glass, handles, and lamp shades. It can even be processed into synthetic fibers used for clothing—rayon.

Resins that exist in nature are used to produce plastics. Asian insects produce a gum-like substance known as shellac, which can be turned into varnish. These early forms of plastics are used to seal wood and other objects with a hard, protective finish. Turpentine, extracted from certain pine trees, can be distilled to form another kind of resin. Plastics made from these resins are easily molded into any shape that can be imagined. Other natural resins, such as asphalt and pitch, are also used in the production of plastics which are used to produce parts for electric motors, dishes, and knobs.

By mixing phenol with coal-tar, formaldehyde, and a few other ingredients, phenol plastics are produced. Tables, cups, plates, bottles, and many of the items necessary to modern everyday life are made from phenol plastics. These plastics are similar to those made from natural resins; however, resins formed in the phenol process are synthetic resins, or substances that do not occur in nature. One of today's largest problems is dealing with disposal of plastics, which help pollute the earth. Researchers and chemists have developed many forms of plastics from synthetic resins. One is a synthetic fiber known as polyester, which is widely used in manufacturing clothing. Vinyl, acrylics, and polystyrenes are all made from synthetic resins. Of all the plastic objects produced today, about thirty percent are made from synthetic resins.

Plastics from milk and soybean proteins are used to make the last form of plastic. Molded into steering wheels, buckles, and beads, these plastics have the texture and durability of natural substances. Synthetic rubber is made from protein plastics. In other forms, these plastics are used to produce clothing that keeps people as warm as natural wool.

14. What is the topic of this report or speech?
   a. modern technology   c. industry
   b. plastics   d. experimentation

15. Why do people need plastics?
   a. to help keep the earth clean of pollution
   b. to help provide the energy sources needed by industry
   c. to help in the manufacture of the goods used in everyday life
   d. to help in preserving the natural substances that occur on the earth

16. What makes the difference among the various types of plastics?
   a. how the plastics themselves are produced   c. how the plastics are disposed of after use
   b. how the plastics are used to make goods   d. how the plastics are able to withstand heat

17. **Why do manufacturers look for cheap materials that can be used to produce goods that will be sold?**
    a. to keep the price of selling goods low
    b. to keep the cost of making goods low
    c. to keep the manufacturing process as short as possible
    d. to keep the amount of money industry needs to borrow as small as possible

18. **One sentence does not add more information about the use of plastics. It should be removed from this report or speech. Which sentence should be removed?**

    _____

    _____

19. **How would life change if plastics were outlawed because of the problems they pose for the environment?**

    _____

    _____

    _____

    _____

    _____

    _____

    _____

Open-Ended
Question

20. **Use a separate piece of paper or write in your literary response journal. Refer to the information in this lesson.**

Most of the discoveries achieved in the 1800s were made by individuals working in private with their own money.

● Why do you think most of the research done today is financed by businesses and the government?

● Why is this work beneficial not only to businesses and government but also to the people of the world?

Extension Activities

Reading Prompt ● Identifying Central Ideas

**Individual
Activity**

21. **Skim various articles in newspapers and magazines or sections of material in your textbooks. What are the topics of these selections? What details help explain these topics? What is the central idea of each selection? Make a list of these topics and central ideas. Explain to the class how successful each writer was in presenting his or her ideas.**

_____

_____

_____

_____

Speaking Prompt ● Elaborating on a Central Idea

**Cooperative
Group
Activity**

22. **Work with a group. Discuss a book or movie that is known by all the members. Talk about the topic of the work, details that help explain or describe this topic, and the central idea intended by the author. How does a discussion of the work's detail help in determining the central idea? Did any of the details lead you to see something in the work that you had not noticed before? In what other ways can group discussion help promote new ideas?**

_____

_____

_____

_____

_____

Writing Prompt ● Using Critical-Thinking Skills

**Workplace
Readiness
Activity**

23. **Work with a group. Talk about the importance of a neat appearance and well-prepared resumé in looking for a job. What does this attention to detail tell a prospective employer? Why do employers look for people who present themselves and their work in an impressive way? How can unnecessary details or the inability to focus on central ideas affect a job interview or the effectiveness of a resumé? What other tips should applicants keep in mind as they look for jobs? Create a booklet of tips people should follow when they are applying for jobs. You may wish to add your booklet as a resource for your school library or media center.**

_____

_____

_____

_____

Classroom Discussion

Do you read to learn or to be entertained? What kind of books provide you with information while at the same time entertaining you? What can you learn by reading a poem or a play?

Classroom Activity

Read the following information and answer the questions in the boxes.

Your assignment is to write about the most remarkable person you've ever met. Your work will be included in a national magazine for teenaged readers. You're also supposed to use an appropriate literary form. In planning your work, you create the following chart of literary forms. A literary form is a way of writing that includes a certain style, length, format, and subject matter.

Name of Literary Form	Description	Fiction or Nonfiction	Example
Novel or Short Story	tells a story in prose; a novel is a long story	usually fiction	*The Color Purple* by Alice Walker (novel)
Personal Essay	tells a writer's thoughts about some topic	nonfiction	"Self-Reliance" by Ralph Waldo Emerson
Drama	tells a story through the actions and words of characters on a stage or on film	usually fiction	"Fences" by August Wilson (play); *Forrest Gump* (film)
Poem	describes a scene, event, memory, or emotion in colorful language; is usually divided into short lines	fiction or nonfiction	"Success" by Emily Dickinson

Step 1

Identify your purpose for writing.

1. What topic will you use for your work?

   _____

2. Who is the audience for your work?

   _____

3. What kind of reaction would you like to get from your audience?

   _____

Step 2

Decide how you will approach your writing assignment.

4. Will your writing be fiction or nonfiction? Why?

   _____

   _____

5. Will you be telling a story; describing a person, event, or emotion; or giving your thoughts on a topic? Explain your answer.

   _____

   _____

6. Should you write formally or in a simple style, as if you were speaking?

   _____

7. Who is the most remarkable person you've met? Briefly describe that person.

   _____

Step 3

Choose the literary form that best fits your assignment.

8. Which literary form is best for describing something, such as a person, scene, or event?

   _____

9. Which literary form is best for giving your personal thoughts on some topic?

   _____

10. Which literary form is best for telling a story through the words and actions of characters on a stage or on film?

    _____

11. Which literary form is best for telling a fictional story in prose?

    _____

12. Which literary form will you use for your assignment? Why?

    _____

Language Arts

Open-Ended Question

13. Think about your answer to this question. Write your answer on the lines. Be prepared to talk about your answer in a classroom discussion. What literary forms do you think will be most popular in the 21st century? Why?

_____

_____

_____

_____

_____

_____

Ideas to Remember

> **literary form**—a way of writing that includes a certain style, length, format, and subject matter
>
> **novel or short story**—a literary form that tells a made-up story in prose
>
> **personal essay**—a literary form in which a writer tells his or her thoughts on some topic
>
> **drama**—a literary form that tells a story through the actions and words of characters on a stage or on film
>
> **poem**—a literary form that describes a scene, event, memory, or emotion in colorful language and is usually divided into short lines

Guided Practice Activity

Each of the following examples tells about the Oklahoma Land Run of 1889 in a different literary form. Identify each literary form. Name several details that helped you to identify it.

14. Tess poked her head out of the covered wagon. There were thousands of people lined up, some in wagons, some in carriages, some on horseback, a few on foot. Tess's father was checking his pocket watch. At exactly noon, a bugle would sound, and the Oklahoma Territory would be opened to settlers. The race would be on to find the best land available. A certain number of people—"Sooners," they were calling them—had sneaked onto the land early and were hiding among the trees or rocks, waiting to stake their claims on the land they'd already chosen. Tess climbed onto the seat of the wagon, between her parents. She was starting to ask a question when the bugle call blared. All at once the air was filled with the dust and thunder from thousands of horses. The Oklahoma Land Run was under way!

Literary form:

_____

Identifying details:

_____

15. On April the twenty-second
In eighteen-eighty-nine
Thousands of hopeful settlers
Trembled at the Kansas line.

Their hearts were beating wildly,
Their heads were filled with dreams,
As the riders spurred their horses
And the drivers raced their teams.

The bugle call was buried
In the hoofbeats and the cries
As thousands of hopeful settlers
Dashed off to start new lives.

Literary form:

_____

Identifying details:

_____

16. *(Setting: A field with trees in the background. A settler named ELIJAH HARRIS is on one knee, pounding a stake into the dirt with a hammer. Suddenly another man in a black straw hat approaches from stage right. He looks angry.)*
MAN IN STRAW HAT: Hey, what do you think you're doing there?
ELIJAH: What does it look like? I'm staking my claim to this land.
MAN IN STRAW HAT: Well, you can just pull that stake outta the ground. This here's my land. I've had it since yesterday morning.
ELIJAH: That's very interesting. Because the territory wasn't opened for settlement until today at noon.
MAN IN STRAW HAT: Makes me no never mind. Here is where I'm going to stay. You know what they do to claim jumpers like you?
ELIJAH *(standing up to show that he's seven inches taller than the man in the hat)*: No, you tell me what they do.

Literary form:

_____

Identifying details:

_____

17. I can still remember those early days of Oklahoma, before statehood. My hometown of Lawton started out as three lemonade stands and a thousand tents run by real estate dealers. Most of those dealers seemed determined to cheat at least one person every hour. Land deeds changed hands faster than the cards in a poker game. In fact, there were plenty of gamblers and "shell game" players to take money from anyone foolish enough to play. I also remember people who were trying to make a more honest living. A woman called "Button Mary" looked for men with buttons

GO TO NEXT PAGE

 Language Arts

missing on their shirts. She would sew a new one on for a dime. A blacksmith with no business suddenly became a dentist. In minutes a long line formed in front of his tent. A Frenchman sold muddy water at a nickel a cup. Some people even earned money by standing in line at the post office. Busy settlers were willing to pay them so as not to waste any time.

Literary form:

_____

Identifying details:

_____

Application Activity

Read the samples of literary form. Then answer the questions that follow.

A.　　The first time I saw Nighthawk Jackson, he was no more than sixteen. This was back in the late twenties. He liked to hang around the joints where the field workers would go to dance at night. Nighthawk loved to watch the blues singers playing their guitars and wailing those sad songs. When they'd take a break, he'd sneak up and strum the guitar strings a few times. Couldn't play a lick. Then he disappeared for about a year. When he came back, he could sing and play guitar like nobody else. He could even play the sound of the wind on his guitar. Now where do you suppose he learned to play like that?

B.　　He sits with his guitar, sits all alone.
His high sweet voice is rising like the moan
Of winter wind that passes through the trees.
He sings a song, and his guitar agrees
With every word. When Nighthawk is in flight,
The blues swirl like fog on a dark night.

C.　　(The scene is a small shack in Mississippi. A blues singer named CHARLIE finishes playing to a small crowd. He stands up to take a break. JIMMY slips over and picks up CHARLIE's guitar.)
CHARLIE: Hey now, son. What are you doing there? Get away from there.
JIMMY (trying to strum the guitar): Mister, I just want to learn.
CHARLIE: That's all very well. But get your own guitar. This one here's my living.
JIMMY: I'll pay for lessons.
CHARLIE (looking at the boy's ragged overalls): Don't figure I'd get rich that way. Maybe some other time, son.

D.　　Jimmy Jackson was sixteen years old when he hopped a freight train to Memphis. He was determined to learn the blues, and everyone said that Memphis was the home of the blues. Jimmy sought out the best blues singers in town. He begged them to teach him, but no one was interested.

　　Finally he met a blind singer named Bones. Sitting on the street corner, playing his guitar for tips, Bones sang the blues in a beautiful high voice. Jimmy would ask him question after question. He would imitate the way Bones placed his fingers on the neck of the guitar. Jimmy bought his own cheap guitar and started to practice. He would practice so late into the evening that Bones started calling him "Nighthawk." After months of practice, Jimmy was ready to go back to Mississippi. He was anxious to show everyone what he'd learned.

GO TO NEXT PAGE

18. **What is the topic for all of these samples? Circle the letter of your answer.**

   a. the history of a music called the blues

   b. a blind singer named Bones

   c. how music in the South has changed over the years

   d. a singer named Nighthawk Jackson playing the blues

19. **Sample A is an example of what literary form? Circle the letter of your answer.**

   a. novel or short story

   b. drama

   c. poem

   d. personal essay

20. **Sample B is an example of what literary form? Circle the letter of your answer.**

   a. novel or short story

   b. drama

   c. poem

   d. personal essay

21. **Sample C is an example of what literary form? Circle the letter of your answer.**

   a. novel or short story

   b. drama

   c. poem

   d. personal essay

22. **Sample D is an example of what literary form? Circle the letter of your answer.**

   a. novel or short story

   b. drama

   c. poem

   d. personal essay

23. **Which sample tells about the characters by showing how they talk? Circle the letter of your answer.**

   a. Sample A

   b. Sample B

   c. Sample C

   d. Sample D

24. **Which sample tries to describe the sound of blues music by using colorful language? Circle the letter of your answer.**

   a. Sample A

   b. Sample B

   c. Sample C

   d. Sample D

25. **Which sample is best for this topic? Explain your answer, using details from the sample.**

   _____

   _____

   _____

   _____

Open-Ended Question

26. Use a separate piece of paper or write in your literary response journal. Refer to the information in this lesson. How do you think the life of a blues singer in the 1930s was different from the life of a pop singer today?

Language Arts

Extension Activities

Individual Activity

Writing Prompt ● Writing in Different Literary Forms

27. **Think of an event in your life that was exciting, funny, scary, or suspenseful. How would you present this event as a play or as a short story? Briefly write the event in four different ways: as a story in prose, as a poem, as a personal essay, and as a drama. Follow the examples in this lesson as you write. Which literary form was best for your tale? Why?**

_____

_____

_____

Cooperative Group Activity

Reading Prompt ● Making a Chart of Poetry Forms

28. **Work with a partner or small group. On a large poster board, make a chart like the one below listing all the poetry forms you can find. Look in the library for books on poetry that list the different forms. Include such foreign forms as the Japanese haiku. You might also include the blues lyric form, like the following:**

   The train left the station with two lights on behind.
   The train left the station with two lights on behind.
   The blue light was my blues and the red light was my mind.

   When you've completed the chart, discuss the different forms. Would some forms be best for certain subjects or moods? See if you can display your chart in the school library in an exhibit on world literature.

Name of Poetry Form	Rules of the Form	Where It Began	Example

Speaking Prompt ● Identify Patterns and Investigate Relationships

Workplace Readiness Activity

29. **Work with a group. Hold a discussion about how different literary forms are used in commercials on TV and radio. For example, some commercials are like miniature plays while others are like personal essays. Talk about specific commercials that are based on some literary form. How is the form used? Is it used mainly for comic effect? How does the form help sell the product or service being advertised? Choose a product and work together to create a commercial for it using one of the literary forms discussed in this lesson. When you're finished, record your commercial on videotape or audio tape and play it for the rest of the class. Encourage the class to identify what literary form was used in the commercial and how effective it was.**

_____

_____

**Classroom
Discussion**

**What kinds of things make up a person's opinions? How are these ideas
different from facts? How can information in a piece of material help you
make decisions about the ideas contained in that material?**

**Classroom
Activity**

Read and examine the information below. Answer the questions that follow.

An audience must make decisions whether they are reading material or listening to a
speech. They must decide which ideas are **facts**, or information that can be proved, and
which ideas are the presenter's **opinions**, or those things the presenter believes or feels.
Conclusions are decisions by the audience, based on facts and opinions, on what to think
about something. Think about these ideas as you read the following selection about the
French Revolution.

Poverty and a desire for freedom turned the people of Paris against their king in 1789.
They formed their own army and managed to arrest the king and his family. A new, freely
elected government was set up, which was charged with the task of spreading the
revolution throughout France and of forming a democratic government. Since all of Europe
was ruled by various monarchs, the revolutionary government had few friends in the
world. Soon, other European countries were at war with the new Republic of France.

Austria's emperor was the brother of the French queen, Marie Antoinette, and he raised
armies to rescue his sister and place the government back in the hands of her husband.
However, Marie Antoinette had never been popular with her French subjects. The queen
refused to follow the strict rules of court life and spent extravagant sums of money on her
lifestyle. It is not surprising that the French people, most of whom lived in poverty, would
hate the queen for using their taxes to live in luxury. In time, the king and queen were
convicted of committing crimes against the people and executed publicly in Paris.

Step 1

Locate the topic
and the central
idea.

1. What is the topic of this material?

_____

2. What is the central idea about the topic?

_____

_____

_____

Step 2

Determine which
details are facts
and which are
opinions.

3. What is a fact?

_____

Language Arts

4. What is an opinion?

_____

5. Which sentence in the paragraphs is the writer's or speaker's opinion?

_____

_____

Step 3

Develop your own conclusion about the topic based on the facts from the material.

6. What opinion did you form about the events of the French Revolution? What facts from the paragraph support your opinion?

Opinion:

_____

_____

Supporting facts:

_____

_____

Open-Ended
Question

7. Think about your answer to the following question. Write your answer on the lines. Be prepared to talk about your answer in a classroom discussion. Do you feel the French people were justified in their treatment of the king and queen? Explain your answer.

_____

_____

_____

_____

_____

_____

Ideas to
Remember

fact–detail that can be proved

opinion–what a writer or speaker thinks or believes about a topic

conclusion–a decision, based on facts and opinions, on what to think about something

Guided Practice Activity

Read and examine the information below. Answer the questions that follow.

Government was not the only institution to be changed by the revolution. The new leaders set up plans to reform society completely. Artists would create paintings and sculptures that would express the ideals of the revolution. Rather than depict the feats of ancient heroes and kings, artists would show the heroism of the French people and its revolutionary leaders. All the systems of measurement were changed as well. The calendar was reorganized and the months were renamed. Volume and length were now to be measured in units of ten instead of twelve. Of all the social changes created during the revolution, only the metric system remains in use today. Exchange of ideas in today's world would be much simpler if the people of the United States would accept that metric system and completely abandon the old system of miles, gallons, and pounds.

Even the French Republic itself came to an end. War with the monarchs of Europe led to the development of a great French army. A French lieutenant from the island of Corsica, Napoleon Bonaparte, showed remarkable skills in handling artillery that led to a great victory that saved the French fleet at Toulon. His subsequent successes led the government to put him at the head of the army. Napoleon's military genius led France to great victories throughout Europe. Finally, Napoleon felt his skills were needed in ruling France. He knew his popularity with all the French people was extraordinarily high, and that hatred and fear of the government spread as thousands lost their lives through executions carried out by the revolutionary government. Napoleon took over the government and developed the Code Napoleon, a plan of laws and government still followed in France today. Soon, the monarchy returned when Napoleon declared himself to be the emperor of France and the territories he had conquered in her name.

Step 1

Locate the topic and the central idea.

8. What is the topic of this material?

_____

9. What is the central idea about the topic?

_____

_____

Step 2

Determine which details are facts and which are opinions.

10. Which sentence in the paragraphs is the writer's or speaker's opinion?

_____

_____

_____

     Language Arts

Step 3

Develop your own conclusion about the topic based on the facts from the material.

11. **What opinion did you form about the events leading to the end of the French Revolution? What facts from the paragraph support your opinion?**

Opinion:

_____

_____

Supporting facts:

_____

_____

Application Activity

Read and examine the information below. Answer the questions that follow.

By 1798 only Great Britain was at war with France. Napoleon decided to lead the French army against Britain's troops in India. This link in the British Empire was deemed to be the weakest, and the Asian colony's great resources would help further enrich France and its emperor. In May, Napoleon led a great fleet of ships to Egypt. The army would establish a base at Alexandria and then move east into Asia. Soon after landing, the French ships were destroyed by the British in the Battle of the Nile.

Napoleon had more in mind than just military conquests in Egypt and Asia. Scientists and artists traveled with the army so they could analyze and research the accomplishments of people who had developed this part of the world. France and, indeed, all of Europe thrilled at the marvelous ideas and reports that were sent back by Napoleon's expedition. Egyptian styles helped bring about a revolution that spread across the continent of Europe.

For centuries, European clothing had been complex and elaborate. Rich materials were used to create elaborately decorated styles of clothing. Men's coats were highly embroidered, sometimes with thread made of fine strands of solid gold. Women wore gowns that exaggerated their figures. Corsets were used to make the women's waists tiny. Frameworks of bone and wood held skirts far out to women's sides. Layers and layers of ruffles, silk, and satin were placed over the frames to create fabulous dresses. The gowns were often so wide that women had to sidle sideways to pass through doorways. Men and women wore wigs that were carefully dusted with perfumed powders. Women's hairstyles were incredibly showy. The wigs were built up in towers of curls that could reach three feet in height. Birds, models of ships and carriages, and other items were often worked into the wigs to form scenes that celebrated current events. Women then topped off these creations with very tall hats. With the wigs and hats, some women were ten feet tall from the soles of their shoes to the tops of their hats. It is hard to imagine all the money that was wasted in purchasing such items that only proved how vain some people can be.

The simple styles of ancient Egyptian dress were a sharp contrast to the fashions of Europe. Plain straight dresses that resembled Egyptian gowns and Greek togas appealed to the revolutionaries of France. These styles were adopted to stress that the new republic would be completely different from the old kingdoms that had dominated the continent. Men's clothes also became simpler. Silk stockings were abandoned and trousers were lengthened. Dark colors and simple lines were used to create coats, shoes, and hats. France had long influenced all the people of Europe, and this phenomena did not change. Britain and all the people of Europe followed suit. These styles even spread across the Atlantic Ocean and became popular in North and South America. Much of the world had experienced a true revolution in fashion.

12. What is the topic of this report or speech?

a. 18th century technology

b. a fashion revolution

c. the wonders of Egypt and Asia

d. Napoleon's conquest of the world

13. What did Napoleon hope to achieve with his expedition to Africa and Asia?

a. conquest of British territory

b. enrichment of France with resources from Africa and Asia

c. knowledge of the history and culture of Africa and Asia

d. all of the above

14. Which word best describes the fashions of Europe in the late 1700s?

a. elaborate

b. inexpensive

c. simple

d. practical

15. Which word best describes the fashions of Europe after the receipt of reports from Napoleon's expedition?

a. elaborate

b. expensive

c. simple

d. showy

16. Why did the people of Europe often follow the ideas and styles of the French?

a. to show that they were rich and powerful

b. to stay in step with trends that become widely admired

c. to hide the poverty of their countries

d. to keep manufacturers successful so jobs were protected

17. One sentence states the writer's or speaker's opinion about the ideas expressed in these paragraphs. Which sentence states an opinion?

_____

_____

18. What changes or events might cause the people of Europe to abandon the new simple styles and adopt a new kind of fashion?

_____

_____

_____

Open-Ended Question

19. Use a separate piece of paper or write in your literary response journal. Refer to the information in this lesson.

   ● How have other revolutions in history affected various governments?

   ● Which of these revolutions also brought about social changes, and how did these changes affect people's lives?

Extension Activities

Viewing Prompt ● Analyzing Styles

Individual Activity

20. Look through an encyclopedia for information about clothing styles and how they have changed over the centuries. What were some of the changes that came about? How did one style seem to affect later styles? When did people seem to turn back to styles that had been popular in the past? What do the changes seem to tell you about changes in people's opinions? What conclusions can you draw about what life must have been like during a particular period by examining fashions of the time? Write a short report expressing your ideas and opinions.

_____

_____

_____

Writing Prompt ● Examining 20th Century Revolutions

Cooperative Group Activity

21. Work with a group. Choose a country or area that has undergone a revolution in the 20th century, such as Russia, India, Poland, Korea, or Indonesia. Research the revolution and its effects. What events led to the revolution? How was the revolution carried out? What form of government was overthrown, and what new form was established? How did life change for people after the revolution? Do you think that the changes were for the better or for the worse? Write a group report that explains your opinions and conclusions.

_____

_____

_____

Speaking Prompt ● Analyzing Technology

Workplace Readiness Activity

22. Work with a group. Talk about the influence of televisions and the world wide web on modern society. How have these media forms influenced people's opinions, styles, and other facets of modern life? What kinds of people who work in the media try to affect people's opinions? What techniques do they use? How are polls used to determine what people's opinions are? Which of these fields are ones that are being considered as career possibilities by members of the group?

_____

_____

Lesson 2C

Drafting: Elaboration and Organization of Ideas (Introduction, Logical Progression of Ideas, and Conclusion)

Classroom Discussion

How does your favorite movie begin? What happens to the characters during the course of the movie? How is the story resolved? Why would you recommend this movie to other people?

Classroom Activity

Read and examine the information below. Answer the questions that follow.

In preparing a report or speech, authors and speakers must catch their audience's attention with an interesting introduction. The details that follow must fit into an order that makes sense and is easy to follow. The conclusion of the work must tie all the details together.

Paragraph A

Mrs. Worral and the local minister arrived the next morning to check further into the background of this amazing visitor. The clothing worn by the young woman was made of good English cloth, but it was sewn into styles only seen in pictures of people who lived in Asia. The minister was familiar with Asia and had brought books on this topic to the interview. Pictures of China interested the young woman, who managed to indicate she knew this land. However, nothing more about her history could be determined. It was a mystery that would have to be solved at a later day. However, people seem to me to be such curious creatures that I believe that the young woman's story was learned eventually.

Paragraph B

Owners of a cottage in Almondsbury, England found they had an unusual guest on the evening of April 3, 1817. They found a young woman on their doorstep. She did not speak a word of English, and did not understand the questions they put to her. By the use of hand signals, she was able finally to let them know that she was seeking a place to spend the night. The surprised people decided to take the matter to a local judge.

Paragraph C

Somehow the amazing woman understood the people's intentions and showed signs of reluctance at having to face the judge. She had to be almost dragged to the home of Mr. and Mrs. Worral, who both made the lady understand that they wanted to see any papers that she might be carrying. All she had on her person were a few personal articles and very little money, but it was all English money. Mrs. Worral arranged for the surprising young woman to be housed in a local inn for the night.

Step 1

Make sure the details in your work are placed in a logical order.

> **1. Examine the events that happened in the story. Which paragraph seems to have events that introduce the story?**
>
> _____

Language Arts

2. Which paragraph describes how the people reacted upon meeting this young woman?

_____

3. Should this paragraph precede or follow the introductory paragraph?

_____

4. According to the order of events that you identified, which paragraph would seem to be the last one in this part of the story?

_____

Step 2

Create an introduction that catches the audience's attention.

5. What is the topic of these paragraphs?

_____

6. What is the main idea about the topic?

_____

_____

7. What would be the focus of your introduction about this topic?

_____

_____

8. A dramatic situation often creates an effective introduction that catches an audience's attention. Which paragraph above would make an effective introduction?

_____

Step 3

Create a conclusion that ties together all the details you wish to present.

9. To develop an effective conclusion, a writer or speaker should sum up the facts and present opinions or make predictions about what will happen next. Which paragraph would be the basis for a strong conclusion for this section?

_____

10. Which part of the conclusion is not only the author's opinion but is also a prediction of what will happen next?

_____

_____

Lesson 2c

Open-Ended Question

11. Think about your answer to the following question. Write your answer on the lines. Be prepared to talk about your answer in a classroom discussion. Why do you think that mystery stories are some of the most popular works to be published and made into films?

_____

_____

_____

_____

_____

_____

Ideas to Remember

introduction–the opening of an essay or report that introduces the topic and grabs the reader's attention

logical progression of ideas–the order of events and details that seems to make sense and is easy to understand

conclusion–the last section of an essay or report that sums up the information and often gives the writer's opinions about the topic or what needs to be done in the future

Guided Practice Activity

Read the next portion of the story that began in the Classroom Activity. Answer the questions that follow.

Paragraph D

What was to happen to this mysterious stranger who was familiar with the people of far distant China? Mrs. Worral decided that the young woman should stay in her own home. The Asian lady was not eager to return to the Worral's home, but she finally agreed to the decision. Mrs. Worral intended to lodge the stranger with the mansion's housekeeper. In further meetings, Mrs. Worral decided to make an important speech that she hoped would settle once and for all if the young woman was a fraud. She carefully explained the trouble and care that were being given to the stranger and the dangers she faced from the courts should she be proven to have tricked the people of the county. All the while, the young woman showed no sign of understanding the speech, but smiled most genially at her new friend. Mrs. Worral was satisfied, spoke her name slowly and clearly, and pointed at herself. The young lady was quick to catch on, so she pointed to herself and said the name *Caraboo*.

Language Arts

Paragraph E

Caraboo's adventures became even more fabulous to the people of England once they knew her true story. Caraboo was a native of an island nation known to no one in England. Jevasu was an island ruled by an Asian king, who was not only Caraboo's ruler but also her father. The young lady was not plain Caraboo, but the Princess Caraboo of an Asian royal family. Pirates had captured the princess and taken her with them on their travels. Once they neared the shores of England, they dropped off their unfortunate prisoner, never once having gained any advantage from the kidnapping. Everyone thrilled at the excitement of the tale, and accepted her as a genuine royal personage. Mrs. Worral could not leave a member of a royal family in a home for the poor, so Princess Caraboo became the permanent guest at Knole, the home of the Worrals. The princess's amazing, and to me unbelievable, adventures at sea were over, but her story would take more amazing turns.

Paragraph F

Since nothing more for Caraboo could be done by Mrs. Worral, the young woman was taken to a local home for the poor. News of the puzzling visitor spread through nearby communities. Crowds of curious people flocked to see Caraboo for themselves. People visiting from foreign lands were brought to meet Caraboo in the hopes that one of them might speak her language. As luck would have it, one of the visitors was Portuguese and knew the Malaysian language. He told the crowds that the language spoken by the exotic Caraboo was similar enough to Malaysian that he could understand simple details of her story.

Step 1

Make sure the details in your work are placed in a logical order.

12. **Examine the events that happened in the story. Which paragraph seems to describe events that introduce this part of the story?**

_____

13. **Which paragraph describes how people reacted as news about the young woman spread?**

_____

14. **Should this paragraph precede or follow the introductory paragraph?**

_____

15. **According to the order of events that you identified, which paragraph would seem to be the last one in this part of the story?**

_____

Step 2

Create an introduction that catches the audience's attention.

16. What is the topic of these paragraphs?

_____

17. What is the main idea about the topic?

_____

_____

_____

18. What would be the focus of your introduction about this topic?

_____

19. A dramatic situation often creates an effective introduction that catches an audience's attention. Which paragraph above would make an effective introduction?

_____

20. What special sentence form is used as the first sentence of the report or speech?

_____

21. Why is this type of sentence an effective one to use in introducing material involving a mystery?

_____

_____

_____

Step 3

Create a conclusion that ties together all the details you wish to present.

22. To develop an effective conclusion, a writer or speaker should sum up the facts and often present opinions or make predictions about what will happen next. Which paragraph would be the basis for a strong conclusion?

_____

23. Which part of the conclusion is not only the author's opinion but is also a prediction of what will happen next?

_____

_____

 Language Arts

Application Activity

Read the sentences below. Then, on the lines provided, rearrange them into three sections: an introduction, a middle section with connected ideas, and a conclusion.

A. Princess Caraboo lived quietly at Knole with the Worrals, who bought her cloth so that she could produce a new wardrobe.

B. This woman confronted Caraboo and claimed that she was really Mary Baker, an ordinary English girl who had worked for years as a maid in different wealthy homes.

C. One last twist of events brought Mary Baker into contact with France's former emperor, Napoleon Bonaparte.

D. Mary's ship had been blown off course, and found itself near St. Helena where Napoleon had been exiled after losing the Battle of Waterloo.

E. Archery was a popular sport in England at the time, which enabled Caraboo to carry a bow and arrow as part of her costume, a tradition she said was honored in her home of Jevasu.

F. Dukes, earls, countesses, and duchesses vied for the honor of hosting the royal princess from Jevasu.

G. After months of worry, Mrs. Worral received news that Princess Caraboo had appeared in Bath, the country's luxurious resort city so popular with the lords and ladies of the land.

H. Since Napoleon never did divorce Princess Marie Louise of Austria, his intentions were never carried out, and no more was ever learned about the fate of Caraboo.

I. Mrs. Worral arrived in Bath to bring Caraboo home just as the strange tale of the young woman was to take a strange twist.

J. This fearless young woman sneaked off the ship in a small boat, rowed herself to shore, led the authorities to believe that she was Princess Caraboo, and demanded to be introduced to the former emperor.

K. There arrived in Bath a woman who was familiar with the tales of Caraboo and the island nation of Jevasu, but she claimed the stories were frauds.

L. The cloth was cut and sewn into fashions that resembled those worn by people of Asia.

M. Caraboo broke down and confessed that these claims were true, but she had only looked for adventure not to steal money or to take advantage of anyone.

N. Mrs. Worral took pity on Mary and helped her book passage on a ship that would take her to a new life in the United States.

O. The dumbfounded British leaders of the island granted her wish, and transported her to the home where Napoleon was being held prisoner.

P. After four months in Almondsbury, the princess suddenly disappeared one quiet night.

Q. Napoleon found her so delightful and charming that he announced his attentions to divorce his wife and marry this Asian princess.

GO TO NEXT PAGE

24.

_____

_____

_____

_____

_____

_____

_____

_____

25.

_____

_____

_____

_____

_____

_____

_____

_____

_____

_____

26.

_____

_____

_____

_____

_____

_____

_____

_____

_____

Language Arts

Open-Ended Question

27. Use a separate piece of paper or write in your literary response journal. Refer to the information in this lesson.

● Would you agree or disagree that Mary Baker must have been a very intelligent person? Why or why not?

● What other qualities did Mary Baker seem to possess? What facts led you to your conclusions?

Extension Activities

Reading Prompt ● Analyzing News Articles

Individual Activity

28. **Skim several articles in a newspaper. Examine the way in which these stories are put together. Look for an introduction, a series of connected ideas in the middle, and a conclusion that ties all the details together. What details are included in the introductory paragraph of each article? How do the other paragraphs explain these details? How does the reporter conclude each article? Write your own conclusion to one article, using your own ideas about the topic.**

_____

_____

Writing Prompt ● Expressing Opinions

Cooperative Group Activity

29. **Work with a group. Choose an issue that is being discussed in your community or state. You may wish to select a topic that is of national interest. Talk about this issue, and allow each member to express an opinion. What seems to be the consensus of your group discussion? Work together to write an essay about this issue. How will you word your introduction to make it effective? What details will you include to support the group's opinions? How will you organize these ideas? How will your conclusion tie together all the ideas and opinions expressed in your essay? Share your paper with other groups in the classroom. Decide which essays are the most effective and the characteristics that made them so effective.**

_____

_____

Speaking Prompt ● Demonstrating Refusal Skills

Workplace Readiness Activity

30. **Work with a group. Discuss the importance of honesty and integrity in the classroom and on the job. Why do teachers and employers value these characteristics? What kinds of temptations might encourage students or employees to violate the trust of their teachers and employers? What can students and employees say and do to show that they will not succumb to temptations that other people may place before them? How can these refusals be worded so that people will know that future temptations are a waste of time? Work up a skit that displays effective ways of using refusal skills? Present your skit for the class or the school. You may wish to videotape your skit and other skits presented by members of your class.**

_____

_____

Classroom Discussion

Do you ever get tired of the same old routine? What kinds of things do you do to keep from falling into a rut? Why do you think people often look for new things to do?

Classroom Activity

Read and examine the information below. Then answer the questions that follow.

Boring an audience is the last thing a writer or speaker wishes to do. After all, the work was completed in the hopes that it would be enjoyed and appreciated. **Varied sentence structure** keeps material from becoming repetitive and boring. Check your work by reading each paragraph. Listen for different sentence sounds. How can you ensure that you have achieved variety in your writing or speeches?

Incorporating Varied Sentence Structures
Break very long sentences into shorter ones in order to create sentences that vary in length. Also remember to combine facts from several short sentences into one compound or complex sentence.
Use words like *and, or, but, nor, not only,* and *but also* to combine two sentences made of independent clauses.
Independent clauses can also be joined by using only a colon or a semicolon.
Words like *since, because, which, that, who, after,* and *while* are used to introduce dependent clauses. Use a comma to combine a dependent clause with an independent clause to create a complex sentence.
Remember that the use of questions and exclamations rather than one long paragraph of simple declarative sentences keeps your work lively and entertaining.
Create a great beginning for a sentence by using descriptive words.
Don't be afraid to experiment with your wording. Keep changing your word order until you achieve an effect that you like.

Paragraph A

People often talk about the land. They say that it is the only thing that lasts. Land can move, though. The earth is covered with a crust. This crust floats on the mantle. It is a layer of molten rock just below the crust. The crust is broken into sections. Each section is a tectonic plate. These plates float on the mantle. They pull away from each other. Sometimes they bump into each other, too. This causes earthquakes. About 200 million years ago, Madagascar was part of Africa. It helped make up the eastern part of this continent. Plate tectonics pulled the land away from Africa. It moved east at a very slow pace. It moved less than an inch each year. Madagascar now is 500 miles to the east of Africa.

Paragraph B

People often say that the land is the only thing that lasts, but the land can move. The earth is covered with a crust, which floats on the mantle. This layer of molten rock just below the crust is broken into sections. Each section is a tectonic plate; these plates float on the mantle. They pull away from each other. However, they sometimes bump into each other, causing earthquakes. About 200 million years ago, Madagascar was part of the eastern continent of Africa. Plate tectonics pulled the land away from Africa. It moved east at a very slow pace, less than an inch each year. Now, Madagascar is 500 miles to the east of Africa.

Step 1

Decide which sentence structures are used in Paragraph A.

1. **Look at the first sentence. How many words were used to create this sentence?**

   _____

2. **How many words make up the second and third sentences?**

   _____

3. **Are there any compound or complex sentences in this sample?** _____

Step 2

Decide which sentence structures are used in Paragraph B.

4. **Which sentence in Paragraph B is exactly like a sentence in Paragraph A?**

   _____

5. **How many words are there in each of the first three sentences in this sample paragraph?**

   _____

6. **What kind of sentences are the first and second sentences in this sample?**

   _____

7. **One in this sample is a compound sentence; it is a sentence with a main clause and a subordinate clause. Which sentence is a compound sentence?**

   _____

Step 3

Identify how
a variety
of sentences
was achieved.

8. **Which paragraph has a better variety of sentence structures?**

_____

9. **What makes the sentences in the other paragraph repetitive?**

_____

10. **Look at the first sentence in Paragraph B. How many sentences from Paragraph A were combined to make this sentence?**

_____

Open-Ended
Question

11. Think about your answer to the following question. Write your answer on the lines. Be prepared to talk about your answer in a classroom discussion. What do you think will happen to the island of Madagascar as more centuries pass? Explain your answer.

_____

_____

_____

_____

_____

_____

_____

_____

_____

Ideas to
Remember

variety of sentence structure–using different sentence lengths, structures, and sounds to make a paragraph more interesting to read

compound sentence–a sentence made up of two independent clauses joined by a conjunction or by a colon or semicolon

complex sentence–a sentence made up of an independent clause and one or more subordinate clauses

word choice–choosing words that are fresh and precise to replace common, weak words

synonyms–words with the same meaning

Language Arts

Guided
Practice
Activity

Varying your choice of words will also make your work more effective. Read and examine the information below. Then answer the questions that follow.

Incorporating Varied Word Choice
One mistake often made by writers and speakers is using some words too often. Replace some words with **synonyms** so that your work does not seem repetitive.
Words that are very common or too general can make your work seem weak. Avoid general words like *building*, and use terms for specific things or ideas, such as *home*, *business*, or *church*. Strong verbs describe the action that occurs. Rather than *walk*, use a verb like *march*, *saunter*, or *lope*. Use a simple word when it makes your work easily understandable. But don't be afraid to use a more precise and colorful word.
Weak modifiers are words such as *very* and *so*. Instead of *very hot*, write *steamy* or *blazing*.

For most of its **time**, trees carpeted Madagascar. The mountains were homes for evergreens, such as pines. In the plains of the west and the slopes of the east stood leafy trees, while **pretty** palms **were** along the coast. After **people** arrived, wood was needed for homes and fires. Open land was needed for farms. Soon the land was **clear**, and now erosion **affects** the land.

Step 1

Replace overused or vague nouns with synonyms.

12. Look at the paragraph. What noun is boldfaced in the first sentence? _____

13. Which of the following synonyms creates a vivid image in the reader's mind? Circle the letter of your answer.

    a. years   b. history   c. past

14. What other noun is boldfaced?

_____

15. What synonyms could you use to replace this noun?

_____

Step 2

Replace overused or weak verbs with synonyms.

16. What verb is boldfaced in the third sentence?

_____

17. Which of the following synonyms creates a vivid image in the reader's mind? Circle the letter of your answer.

a. lived   b. thrived   c. grew

18. What other verb is boldfaced?

_____

19. What synonyms could you use to replace this verb?

_____

Step 3

Replace overused or weak modifiers with synonyms.

20. What adjective is boldfaced in the third sentence?

_____

21. Which of the following synonyms creates a vivid image in the reader's mind? Circle the letter of your answer.

a. exotic   b. beautiful   c. cute

22. What other adjective is boldfaced?

_____

23. What synonyms could you use to replace this verb?

_____

Application Activity

Read the paragraphs below. Then answer the questions that follow.

A unique experiment began in the late 1700s on Madagascar. Much of Mexico was a dry and desert area just like Madagascar had become, but the land was still able to produce crops. The secret was Mexico's prickly pear cactus; a plant that stores water inside its pulpy trunk and leaves for later use. The prickly pear was planted in southern Madagascar in 1796. Whenever rain fell, the cacti not only stored water inside themselves, but they helped trap water in the soil itself. Agriculture quickly became a major livelihood in this region of Madagascar.

Conditions went well in southern Madagascar for about 130 years. Then in 1925 another experiment was tried. The Mexican cochineal insect is raised so that its shell can be used to make a brilliant red dye. Since the Mexican prickly pear had been such a success, the cochineal was introduced into Madagascar. Tragedy struck when these insects devoured every prickly pear. Over the next two years, crops died, ponds disappeared, people and cattle died, and the land returned to desert.

      Language Arts

People also harmed Madagascar's animal life. Crocodiles lived in all Madagascar's rivers. These mean animals often hurt people. These people used the rivers. People began hunting the crocodiles. People used crocodiles for food. They used crocodile skins to make leather. Few crocodiles now live in Madagascar's rivers and streams. People do not harm crocodiles in a lake near Anivarano Nord. This is a small town in southern Madagascar. Legend says that a stranger once came to Anivarano Nord. He wanted a drink of water. No one would give him one. One woman was kind enough to give him a drink. The person used magic to make a lake cover the town. All the people became crocodiles. Only the kind woman was left.

24. **Which two paragraphs have a varied sentence structures? Circle your answers.**

a. Paragraph 1   b. Paragraph 2   c. Paragraph 3

25. **What kinds of sentences are used in these paragraphs?**

_____

26. **Which paragraphs have varied word choices? Circle your answers.**

a. Paragraph 1   b. Paragraph 2   c. Paragraph 3

27. **Look at the last paragraph. What noun is used seven times? Circle your answer.**

a. town   b. people   c. Madagascar

28. **What are some synonyms you could use to replace this overused word?**

_____

_____

29. **What synonyms for Madagascar could help vary the word choice by using words that describe the kind of place that it is?**

_____

_____

30. **Which paragraph does not have varied sentence structures and varied word choices? Use the lines below to rewrite this paragraph. Use a variety of sentence structures and a variety of word choices.**

_____

_____

_____

_____

_____

_____

_____

Open-Ended Question

31. Use a separate piece of paper or write in your literary response journal. Refer to the information in this lesson.

- How might the people of Madagascar help bring back agriculture to the southern part of the island?

- Why do you feel it is a good idea or a bad idea for people to attempt changes in the ecology of an area?

Extension Activities

Reading Prompt ● Examining Writing

Individual Activity

32. Skim some of the periodicals that are available in your school library or media center. How effective is the writing in the various articles? What kinds of changes could be made to improve the writing? What makes some of the articles more effective than others? Choose one article, and rewrite it using varied sentence structures and varied word choices. Share your work with the class.

_____

_____

_____

Listening Prompt ● Reviewing a Broadcast

Cooperative Group Activity

33. Work with a partner. Listen to a group or panel discussion on the radio or television. Which speakers made a good impression on you and the studio audience? How did these people make such a good impression? Which of these techniques would help improve your speaking abilities? Work with other pairs of students to hold a panel discussion about the qualities that make a person a good public speaker.

_____

_____

_____

Writing Prompt ● Analyzing Job Opportunities

Workplace Readiness Activity

34. Work with a group. List the careers that are being considered by the members of the group. What kinds of educations are required for these careers? How great will the demand be for these careers in the future? What kinds of salaries can employees expect to earn in these careers? Will it be necessary for people to relocate in order to pursue these jobs? Where are these locations? If necessary, talk to your guidance counselor in order to answer these questions. Write brief reports about each career that you discuss. Remember to use varied sentence structures and varied word choices.

_____

_____

_____

56   Language Arts

Lesson 4A

Editing: Use of Conventions of Print (Grammatical Conventions)

How do signs help drivers find their routes? Why are highway signs used to promote traffic safety? What other kinds of symbols do you deal with on a daily basis?

Classroom Activity

Read and examine the following information. Answer the questions that follow.

Checking over your work to make sure that there are no mistakes is the process of editing. What should you keep in mind as you carry out the editing process?

- **Punctuate sentences made of dependent and independent clauses with commas and semicolons:**

  Winter is the best time of the year, **and** this season means it's time for skiing. (two independent clauses joined with a comma and a conjunction)

  Always be on time; remember to bring all your gear. (two independent clauses joined with a semicolon)

  Since I was nine years old, I have been a part of a baseball team. (one dependent and one independent clause joined with a comma)

  My favorite sport is football, **so I never miss a Sunday NFL game**. (one independent and one dependent clause joined with a comma)

  If you miss too many practice sessions, you will not be allowed to play on game day. (one dependent and one independent clause joined with a comma)

- **Punctuate parenthetical expressions with commas:**

  Gladys Takamoto, **the president of the company**, is interviewing people for the job of her assistant.

  All the copies of that book, **as luck would have it,** were sold out on the first day.

  Have you been waiting long to see the doctor, **Jenny**?

  Hurry up, we will be on time if we run the last few blocks.

- **Make the number of subjects and verbs agree:**

  Mice used in our experiment **run** the maze without danger of harm.

  Each **member** of the track team **runs** the 100-meter race in record time.

  Houses near the library **sell** more easily than any other location in town.

- **Use the proper case for all pronouns:**

    The winners of the contest were Maria and **I**. (nominative case for predicate pronouns)

    Maria and **I** are the only Hopi Indians attending this college. (nominative case for subjects)

    Maria and Sally were invited by **them** to attend the afternoon concert. (objective case for objects of pronouns)

    Maria and Sally took **them** to dinner as a way of saying thank you. (objective case for direct objects)

- **Make pronouns and their antecedents agree in number:**

    If **Linda Snowfall** places a painting in a gallery, **she** knows that her fans will line up on **her** opening day. (Singular form *she* and *her* refers to *Linda Snowfall*.)

    Native American **artists** who display **their** work in Europe are sure to draw big crowds. (Plural form *their* refers to *artists*.)

Madagascar was a deserted island, and then settlers arrived about 400 A.D. Africa was only 500 miles away, but these immigrants were from Asia and Melanesia, islands in the Pacific Ocean. The Malagasy, as the inhabitants are known, were divided into different warring groups. A warrior king finally united them in 1797. Arabs from Africa reached Madagascar about 900; they set up trading communities along the coast. Europeans first made contact with Madagascar in 1500, when Portuguese explorers who were trying to reach China arrived. In time, French colonies were established in Madagascar.

Step 1

Use commas and semicolons to join dependent and independent clauses.

1. **Look at the first sentence in the paragraph. What punctuation mark and conjunction is used to divide these two independent clauses?**

    _____

2. **Look at the sixth sentence. What kinds of clauses make up this sentence?**

    _____

3. **How were these two clauses combined?**

    _____

4. **In which sentence were two independent clauses joined without the use of a conjunction?**

    _____

    _____

5. **How were these two clauses combined?**

    _____

GO TO NEXT PAGE

Language Arts

Step 2

Use commas to set off parenthetical expressions.

6. What parenthetical expression is a part of the second sentence?

_____

7. To what noun does this expression refer?

_____

8. What sets off this expression from the rest of the sentence?

_____

9. What other parenthetical expression is set off with commas?

_____

10. To whom does this expression refer?

_____

Step 3

Check that subjects and verbs agree in number.

11. Look at the second sentence. It has two independent clauses. What is the subject of the first clause?

_____

12. Does the subject require a singular or a plural verb?

_____

13. Look at the second independent clause in this sentence. Does the subject require a singular or a plural verb?

_____

Step 4

Check that the proper case of each pronoun is used.

14. What nominative case pronoun is used in this paragraph?

_____

15. To what noun does this pronoun refer?

_____

16. What objective case pronoun is used in this paragraph?

_____

17. To what noun does this pronoun refer?

_____

59

Step 5

Check that the pronouns agree with their antecedents.

18. Are the nominative case pronoun and object case pronouns singular or plural?

_____

19. To what nouns does *they* refer? Are the nouns singular or plural?

_____

_____

Open-Ended Question

20. Think about your answer to the following question. Write your answer on the lines. Be prepared to talk about your answer in a classroom discussion. What might have kept people from Africa from being the first to reach Madagascar?

_____

_____

_____

_____

_____

_____

_____

_____

_____

_____

Ideas to Remember

complex sentence–a sentence composed of two independent clauses combined through the use of a comma and a conjunction, or through the use of a semicolon

compound sentence–a sentence composed of one independent clause joined with a dependent clause through the use of a semicolon

subject-verb agreement–the rule by which the number of a subject (singular or plural) matches the number of a verb

proper case of a pronoun–the rule by which the case of a pronoun (subjective or objective) is determined by its place in the sentence

pronoun agreement with an antecedent–the rule by which the number of a pronoun must agree with the number of the noun to which it refers

 Language Arts

Guided Practice Activity

Read and examine the following paragraph. Then answer the questions that follow.

Many groups live on this island; the Merina set up the first large kingdom in 1797. King Andrianampoinimerina used weapons bought from French settlers to take control of the island; except for small areas in the west and south. He died in 1810; so King Radama inherited the throne from him. Radama, son of the king, worked with the British to achieve the dream of a united Madagascar. The fight even turned against the French, and them were forced to leave, except for one small trading village. French settlers still live in this island nation and they is the largest foreign group living in Madagascar.

Step 1

Use commas and semicolons to join dependent and independent clauses.

21. Is the first sentence a complex or compound sentence? How are the clauses joined?

_____

_____

22. Is the sentence punctuated correctly? Circle your answer.

yes   no

23. Is the third sentence a compound or complex sentence? How do you know?

_____

_____

24. Is the sentence punctuated correctly? Circle your answer.

yes   no

If no, rewrite the sentence so that it is correct.

_____

_____

Step 2

Use commas to set off parenthetical expressions.

25. What two parenthetical expressions are a part of this paragraph?

_____

_____

26. Which expression is not correctly punctuated? Rewrite the sentence so that it is correct.

_____

_____

Lesson 4_A

Step 3

Check that subjects and verbs agree in number.

27. What is the subject of the last sentence in this paragraph?

_____

28. Does the subject require a singular or a plural verb?

_____

29. What is the verb in this sentence?

_____

30. Does the subject agree with the verb? Circle your answer.

yes   no

If no, rewrite the sentence so that it is correct.

_____

_____

Step 4

Check that the proper case of each pronoun is used.

31. What pronoun cases are used in the third sentence?

_____

32. Are they used as the subject of the sentence or as objects?

_____

33. Is the pronoun correctly used in this sentence?

yes   no

If no, rewrite the sentence so that it is correct.

_____

_____

Step 5

Check that the pronouns agree with their antecedents.

34. What pronouns are used in this paragraph? Are they singular or plural?

_____

35. To what noun does each pronoun refer?

_____

                    Language Arts

36. Which pronoun is used incorrectly? Rewrite the sentence so that it is correct.

_____

_____

Application Activity

Read the following sentences. Decide which sentences need correcting. Rewrite them on the lines.

37. King Radama with British help began a program of Europeanizing his kingdom.

_____

38. The nation was shocked in 1828, when the king died suddenly.

_____

39. Conditions surrounding the death were suspicious, some people felt him were murdered by his wife Ranavalona.

_____

_____

40. Queen Ranavalona turned against European ideas so all of they were driven from the island.

_____

41. Ranavalona turned against the Malagasy and her executed thousands who disagreed with she.

_____

42. This vicious queen gained a nickname, Ranavalona the Terrible.

_____

43. The kingdom was very strong and they even stopped an invasion by western army of British and French troops in 1845.

_____

_____

44. Over a million Malagasy was killed by the time Ranavalona died in 1861, when the new king Radama II turned back to the ideas of King Radama I.

_____

_____

Open-Ended Question

45. Use a separate piece of paper or write in your literary response journal. **Refer to the information in this lesson.**

- What qualities do you think people should look for when choosing a leader, such as a president?

- Do you agree or disagree that voting is a responsibility that no citizen should avoid? Why?

Extension Activities

Listening Prompt ● Analyzing Speech

Individual Activity

46. Listen to the speech of characters in your favorite television program. Jot down a portion of this speech. Turn your notes into a short script. Make sure that you follow the ideas of grammatical conventions as you work. Share your script with the class.

_____

_____

_____

_____

Writing Prompt ● Revising Student Writing

Cooperative Group Activity

47. Work with a partner. Write four or five sentences each about your favorite way to spend your time during the summer. Make sure that you use compound and complex sentences. Include parenthetical expressions and pronouns wherever possible. Place mistakes in each sentence for your partner to catch. Trade papers and revise each other's work.

_____

_____

_____

_____

Speaking Prompt ● Describing Personal Skills for Successful Careers

Workplace Readiness Activity

48. Work with a group. Talk about the skills and qualifications that employers look for when hiring people to fill jobs. Why is each skill important? How are these skills used in various jobs? Why would a sound knowledge of the grammatical conventions be an asset that employers value? Why would these skills be important in jobs that require little writing? Discuss ways in which students can strengthen their employability skills.

_____

_____

_____

_____

Language Arts

Lesson 4B

Classroom Discussion

Have you ever described someone as having a "sunny" outlook? Or being "like a bull in a china shop"? What do these descriptions mean? Why are they more interesting than describing a person in an ordinary style?

Classroom Activity

Read the following information. Then answer the questions in the boxes.

As you edit your work, check your use of **figures of speech**. These are literary devices that describe things in imaginative and colorful ways. Three common figures of speech are simile, metaphor, and idiom.

Figures of Speech		
Name	**Definition**	**Examples**
Simile	a comparison using the words "like" or "as"	● Coach Harris barked **like an angry dog** each time one of us made a mistake. ● The touch of her hand on my arm **was as delicate as a rose petal.**
Metaphor	a comparison that describes something as if it were something else	● That D on today's test **is a warning siren** that I need to study more. ● Last night's snowfall **was a thick white blanket** that covered the neighborhood.
Idiom	a phrase that has a meaning other than the plain meaning of its words	● When Mom saw the scratch on the dining room table, she **hit the ceiling**. (Mom was very angry.) ● Once he was living alone, he had to **keep house** for himself.

Read the following sentences. Refer to them as you answer the questions in the boxes.

A. The news that my grandparents are coming to visit warmed me like a sudden ray of sunshine.

B. Mrs. Brock was a tower of strength when I needed her support at school.

C. Our pitcher threw out his arm and had to take a week off.

GO TO NEXT PAGE

Lesson 4B

Step 1

Identify a simile.

1. **What is a simile?**

_____

2. **Look at sentence A. What two things are being compared in this sentence?**

_____

3. **How does the speaker in the sentence feel when he/she hears the news?**

_____

4. **Does this comparison use the word "like" or "as"? If so, which one?**

_____

5. **What words in sentence A form a simile?**

_____

6. **In your own words, describe how the speaker feels when hearing the news that his or her grandparents are coming to visit.**

_____

Step 2

Identify a metaphor.

7. **What is a metaphor?**

_____

8. **Look at sentence B. What two things are being compared in this sentence?**

_____

9. **Does this comparison use the words "like" or "as"?**

_____

10. **What words in sentence B form a metaphor?**

_____

11. **How does the speaker of the sentence think about Mrs. Brock and what she did?**

_____

Lesson 4B

Step 3

Identify an idiom.

12. What is an idiom?

_____

13. Look at sentence C. What is the ordinary meaning of "throwing something out"?

_____

14. What does the idiom "threw out his arm" mean?

_____

15. Rewrite sentence C, replacing the idiom with your own words.

_____

Open-Ended Question

16. Think about your answer to this question. Write your answer on the lines. Be prepared to talk about your answer in a classroom discussion. How would you translate an idiom in English into another language like Spanish?

_____

_____

_____

_____

_____

_____

_____

_____

_____

_____

Ideas to Remember

figures of speech–literary devices used to describe things in imaginative and colorful ways

simile–a comparison using the words "like" or "as"

metaphor–a comparison describing something as if it were something else

idiom–a phrase that has a meaning other than the plain meaning of its words

Guided Practice Activity

Each of the sentences below contains a figure of speech. Underscore the figure of speech. Then, on the line below the sentence, tell whether the figure of speech is a simile, metaphor, or idiom.

17. **The way Joel smacks his lips when he eats gets under my skin.**

   _____

18. **Like a playful child, the wind blew her straw hat into the swimming pool.**

   _____

19. **Lucinda gave herself away when she accidentally mentioned the surprise party.**

   _____

20. **Judging by the way she reacts to pressure, Madeline must have ice in her veins.**

   _____

21. **The school year has been one long blizzard of tests, reports, and homework assignments.**

   _____

22. **The canyon was as dark and mysterious as an abandoned room in an old house.**

   _____

23. **Despite all our efforts to save the business, it was a battered ship that no one could keep from sinking.**

   _____

24. **We only have half a loaf of bread and some salami, but I think we can scrape by for today's lunch.**

   _____

Application Activity

Read the samples of literary form. Then answer the questions that follow.

Joshua Tree National Park in southern California is a patchwork quilt of trees, rocks, dunes, and flowers. The summer temperature there reaches 120° regularly. There is little water and the landscape can seem harsh at first. Like a hand squeezing a sponge, the desert can dry out even the hardiest hiker. But after a while the stark beauty of the place starts to get under your skin. Some people become so fond of the desert that they come back every year, despite the heat and the hardships.

The animals, plants, and rocks in Joshua Tree National Park are full of surprises. Ocotillo bushes spurt out of the ground like fingers of dark red flame. The Joshua trees are high priests lifting their arms to the sky, begging for rain. Slabs of sheer rock, such as Headstone Rock, rise high into the air. Tortoises, lizards, and rattlesnakes creep slowly along the sand and rock. In the desert, history has been put on hold. And in the light of a red sunset, the desert can be as beautiful as an old painting seen for the first time.

GO TO NEXT PAGE

Language Arts

25. What is Joshua Tree National Park compared to in the first sentence of the first paragraph?

a. trees, rocks, dunes, and flowers

b. a patchwork quilt

c. southern California

d. a harsh landscape

26. What kind of figure of speech is this?

a. simile

b. idiom

c. metaphor

d. personification

27. What is the figure of speech in the third sentence of the first paragraph?

a. like a hand

b. like a hand squeezing a sponge

c. the desert can dry out

d. even the hardiest hiker

28. What kind of figure of speech is this?

a. simile

b. idiom

c. metaphor

d. hyperbole

29. What is the figure of speech in the fifth sentence of the first paragraph?

a. after a while

b. the stark beauty

c. the stark beauty of the place

d. get under your skin

30. What kind of figure of speech is this?

a. simile

b. idiom

c. metaphor

d. personification

31. Find two similes, a metaphor, and an idiom in the second paragraph. Write the sentences below. Underline each figure of speech and tell what kind it is.

_____

_____

_____

_____

_____

_____

_____

_____

Open-Ended Question

32. Use a separate piece of paper or write in your literary response journal. Refer to the information in this lesson. Why do you think the U.S. government expanded the area of California desert that is protected by law?

Extension Activities

Viewing Prompt ● Collecting Figures of Speech from Advertising

Individual Activity

33. **Watch television commercials, listen to radio advertisements, or go through newspaper and magazine ads to collect figures of speech. You might also find examples in advertisements on billboards or in subway cars. Notice how each figure of speech makes the ad more colorful, humorous, or appealing. Note down the figures of speech you find in a chart like the one below. Be prepared to discuss these uses of language in a class discussion.**

TV or Radio Commercial	Figure of Speech	Meaning of the Figure of Speech

Writing Prompt ● Using Figures of Speech to Describe Paintings

Cooperative Group Activity

34. **Work with a partner or small group. Go to the library and find several books containing reproductions of classic paintings by artists such as Claude Monet, Pierre Renoir, Diego Rivera, and Georgia O'Keeffe. Work together to write a paragraph describing each painting that interests you. Use a variety of similes and metaphors in your descriptions. Describe colors, shapes, lighting effects, and the moods of the paintings. If possible, use an opaque projector to display the paintings to your class as you read your paragraph aloud. See if your audience can identify the figures of speech in your work.**

Speaking Prompt ● Identify Personal Interests, Abilities, and Skills

Workplace Readiness Activity

35. **Work with a group. Discuss why employers want to know about the personal interests and proven abilities of people who are applying for a job. Talk about your own interests and skills, and how they would make you a more valuable employee. Where on a job application or resumé would you mention your interests and abilities? How much detail should you go into about these things? How would you describe your interests and abilities in a job interview? Could you use figures of speech to describe what you are best at and what interests you most? Set up a mock job interview and role-play the parts. When you role-play the job applicant, try to concentrate on the abilities that would interest this employer the most.**

Classroom Discussion

What novel or story have you read recently in which there were clues to the ending? How did you use those clues to predict what would happen? Why are stories that end with a "twist" so popular? What do these stories tell you about life?

Classroom Activity

Read the following information about three literary devices. Then answer the questions in the boxes.

Symbolism is a literary device in which an object, person, or place represents a strong feeling or emotion. For example, a bridge might be a symbol for peace between two families or towns that have been feuding. Look for another example of symbolism in the following paragraph.

A. Miko had just moved to a distant city to begin a new career. She was illustrating books for children. One day she received a small package in the mail. Inside was a present from her father: a fine horsehair brush used for watercolor painting. In Miko's family the brush had been passed down from generation to generation for more than a century. It reminded her of hard work and dedication to one's craft. She couldn't have received a more beautiful gift.

Foreshadowing is a literary device in which details are carefully placed in a story to prepare the reader for some important event to come. For example, a character might stumble upon a secret passageway in an old house. Later in the story, the same character uses the passageway to escape from the house. The mention of the passageway foreshadowed its use in the plot. Look for the foreshadowing in the following paragraph.

B. On his way home, Howie would stop off and watch the Rangers soccer team finish their practice. The Rangers were all bigger and faster than the players on Howie's team. The game was going to be a mismatch. Then Howie noticed something. The Rangers' goalkeeper always dove to his right when he had to guess which way the shot was coming. Maybe Howie's teammates should hear about this.

Irony is a literary device that emphasizes the difference between the actual outcome of events and the expected outcome. For example, in O. Henry's "The Gift of the Magi," a girl with beautiful long hair cuts it off and sells it to buy her husband a gold chain for his watch. However, unknown to her, the husband has sold his watch to buy gold combs for her hair. Find the example of irony in the following paragraph.

C. Near-sighted Mr. Pennypacker had saved his meager salary for years. Finally he saved enough to go away on vacation for a whole month. He rented a remote cabin in the mountains with no telephones for miles. All he wanted to do was read. It was his dream to sit quietly and read for hours on end. He unlocked the door to the little cabin and hauled in his suitcase filled with books. As he fumbled for the light switch, his glasses slipped off and fell to the floor. He took a clumsy step and heard a sickening crunch.

Step 1

Identify the use of
symbolism.

1. What is symbolism?

2. In paragraph A, what object is used as a symbol?

3. Why is the object important to Miko?

4. What does the object represent for Miko?

Step 2

Identify the use of
foreshadowing.

5. What is foreshadowing?

6. In paragraph B, what event do you think is being foreshadowed?

7. How do you know that Howie's team is going to play the Rangers?

8. Why is the Rangers team favored over Howie's team?

9. What details foreshadow the event you described in question 6?

Step 3

Identify the use
of irony.

10. What is irony?

Language Arts

11. **In paragraph C, what details did you learn about Mr. Pennypacker?**

_____

_____

12. **What do you expect to happen when Mr. Pennypacker goes up to his cabin?**

_____

13. **What is ironic about Mr. Pennypacker stepping on his glasses?**

_____

14. **Write another ending to this story that is ironic.**

_____

_____

_____

Open-Ended Question

15. Think about your answer to this question. Write your answer on the lines. Be prepared to talk about your answer in a classroom discussion. How can a writer use foreshadowing to create suspense in a story?

_____

_____

_____

_____

_____

_____

_____

_____

Ideas to Remember

symbolism–a literary device in which an object, person, or place represents a strong feeling or emotion

foreshadowing–a literary device in which details are carefully placed in a story to prepare the reader for some important event to come

irony–a literary device that emphasizes the difference between the actual outcome of events and the expected outcome

Guided
Practice
Activity

Read each of the paragraphs below. Then follow the steps and answer the questions in the boxes.

D. The rickety old school bus pulled out early on Saturday morning. It was the day of the annual science class field trip. Dolores hated to miss a Saturday working on car engines with her Dad. She sat on the bus and refused to speak to anyone. The coughing of the bus engine just reminded her of how much fun she could be having at home. This trip would be a terrible bore.

E. For months Leetha's mom had been telling her to go to the eye doctor. The way Leetha squinted her eyes at things, it was obvious she wasn't seeing well. However, Leetha refused to admit that her eyes were bad. Finally, Leetha agreed to visit the eye doctor. She showed up late and moped through the appointment. When she received her new glasses, she put them on and was delighted to see a nice new boy from her high school sitting next to her. "I wave to you in class, but I don't think you've seen me," he said.

F. Vaughn loved to visit his grandparents' house in the country. It had begun as a small woodframe home, as plain as a box. But then Grandpa and Grandma Rushing had begun adding things. It seemed as if every summer there was a new room added on or a garage or a porch. The little house reminded him of his grandparents' enthusiasm for life. When they became gardeners, they built a greenhouse. A love of books led them to build a library room. The house expanded in every direction just like a person's full life.

Step 1

Identify the use of symbolism.

> **15. Which paragraph features an example of symbolism?**
> _____
>
> **16. Is the symbol an object, person, or place?**
> _____
>
> **17. What is the symbol?**
> _____
>
> **18. What does the symbol represent in the paragraph?**
> _____
>
> **19. What details add to the symbol's meaning?**
> _____
> _____
> _____

Lesson 4c

Step 2

Identify the use of foreshadowing.

20. **Which paragraph features an example of foreshadowing?**

_____

21. **What event do you think is being foreshadowed?**

_____

22. **What details foreshadow the event?**

_____

_____

Step 3

Identify the use of irony.

23. **Which paragraph features an example of irony?**

_____

24. **What is ironic about the situation in this paragraph?**

_____

_____

_____

25. **Why is the outcome of the situation unexpected?**

_____

_____

26. **What is ironic about the last sentence of the paragraph?**

_____

_____

_____

Application Activity

Read each paragraph. Choose which kind of literary device it contains and circle it. Then answer the questions that follow the paragraphs.

27. In his most famous poem, the Russian writer Alexander Pushkin described a tragic duel in the snow. He pictured the grey skies, the snowy fields, and the two men facing off with loaded pistols. The hero of his story, Eugene Onegin, shoots and kills a poet named Lensky. All of Russia talked about this famous fictional duel. Years later, Pushkin became involved in a dispute with a French military officer in St. Petersburg. Pushkin challenged the officer to a duel. They met in the snowy fields outside the city. The two men faced each other with loaded pistols. The French officer fired and Pushkin received a mortal wound, just like the poet in his story.

symbolism   foreshadowing   irony

GO TO NEXT PAGE

28. There's a box under Cynthia Delgado's bed. Inside the box is a fairy godmother's white silk costume, made to fit a six-year-old. The costume is complete with a magic wand and a shining gold headband. Cynthia's mother made it for her for a Halloween party long ago. Her mother was just learning to sew. The seams are not particularly straight and the zipper doesn't work too well. However, to Cynthia, the costume is to be treasured forever. To her, it represents how much her mother loves her and all the sacrifices of time and effort she's made over the years.

symbolism   foreshadowing   irony

29. When Garry was in junior high, he and his friends would gather at his house after school. The guys loved to hear his jokes. He would tell them stories using lots of different funny voices. Sometimes they would tape-record interviews, with Garry doing impressions of movie stars. Garry's friends told him he was as funny as the comedians on TV. Now and then, Garry would think about becoming a professional comedian. Then he'd smile to himself and shake his head. No, the thought was too far-fetched. Breaking into show business was just a dream.

symbolism   foreshadowing   irony

30. What is the symbol used in the paragraph that features symbolism?

_____

31. What does this symbol represent?

_____

32. What event is being foreshadowed in the paragraph that features foreshadowing?

_____

33. What details help foreshadow this event?

_____

_____

34. What is ironic in the paragraph that features irony?

_____

_____

35. What details add to the irony?

_____

_____

Open-Ended Question

36. Use a separate piece of paper or write in your literary response journal. Refer to the information in this lesson. What symbol is featured in a movie that you've seen recently? What does the symbol represent?

                    Language Arts

Extension Activities

Writing Prompt ● Noting Examples of Foreshadowing

Individual Activity

37. **Think of several novels, stories, movies, or TV shows that you've read or seen recently. How were later events foreshadowed in the early sections of these works? Did you notice the foreshadowing as you read or watched, or did you only notice it at the end? Did the foreshadowing improve each work? If so, how? Complete a chart like the following to show the examples of foreshadowing you've found.**

Name of Work
What was foreshadowed?
How did the foreshadowing prepare the way for a later event?
How effective was the foreshadowing?

Speaking Prompt ● The Symbol for Your State

Cooperative Group Activity

38. **Work with a group. Discuss what the symbol of your state is. Why does it represent your state in the public's mind? What other symbol could you find for your state? It can be a person, an animal or plant, a place, or an object. Call for suggestions from the group. Discuss each suggestion in detail. Have the person who suggested it explain what feelings and emotions the symbol would call up for the people in your state. Choose the best suggestion and bring it to the full class. Make an illustration or a photocopy of a photograph to present the symbol to your class. Hold a class discussion about the new state symbol you've chosen.**

Speaking Prompt ● Demonstrate Respect for People of Different Races, Ages, Religions, Ethnicity, and Gender

Workplace Readiness Activity

39. **Work with a group. Discuss the struggles that people of different races, ethnic groups, or religions have gone through to achieve success in the United States. Have different members of the group tell stories they've read or heard about these struggles. As a group, do research in the library or on the Internet to prepare a program about the efforts of various minority groups to achieve equality. Use elements of foreshadowing and symbolism in the reports you prepare for the program. For example, explain how Rosa Parks' refusal to move to the back of a bus in Montgomery, Alabama, foreshadowed the larger efforts of the civil rights movement and more widespread protests in the 1960s. Present your program to the class or to a larger gathering of students. Hold a discussion afterward in which the audience can share their own views.**

If you are going to write a report or speech, do you have all the knowledge and information to do the writing, or do you need to use information from other sources? If you use other sources, should you take credit for the information yourself, or should you give credit to the author who wrote the source that you used?

Read and examine the information below. Then answer the questions that follow.

When writing a speech or a report, you usually must use information from other sources. However, you should use your own words when you include this information in your work because it is illegal to copy directly from your sources. Use the ideas from your sources, but write them in your own words. You may quote directly from a source if you use only a few words and acknowledge that you are copying. Read the samples to determine how to use material from sources without copying and how to acknowledge your source.

Source: Lovell, Leah, "The Charming Tales of Beatrix Potter," *International Writers Magazine*, **April '95.**

Beatrix Potter, born in London in 1866, lived much of her life in her parents' home in the city, but eventually moved to the north country where she became a farmer, buying up over 4,000 acres of farmland. While in her parents' home, Miss Potter lived in the nursery, where she developed a love of studying the animals she found in hedgerows, such as rabbits, hedgehogs, squirrels, and frogs. Her first book, *The Tale of Peter Rabbit*, was published in 1900. She eventually became engaged to Peter Warne, the son of her publisher. A few months after their engagement, Peter died suddenly, and Beatrix moved to her first farm, Hill Top. She used the money from publishing other children's book to enlarge her land holdings. She eventually married William Heelis. As a middle-aged farm wife, she became an authority on breeding and raising sheep, and was the first and last woman president of the Herdwick Sheepbreeders' Association. Wishing to preserve farm life and her land, she bequeathed her farms to the National Trust of England. Her original farmhouse is kept as it was when she lived in it. Her hundreds of watercolor paintings reside in museums such as the Tate, the Victoria and Albert Museum, the British National Trust, and in private collections. Beatrix Potter will always be remembered as the writer and illustrator of children's stories, but her contributions to the preservation of her country's history are too many to number.

Report (based on facts from the magazine article)

Beatrix Potter is best known for her children's book *The Tale of Peter Rabbit*. The book has been cherished by generations of children for almost one hundred years. Its author led what many people would consider a sad life during the early part of her life. In her later life, she became a farmer and sheep breeder. Miss Potter lived in her parents' home until her mid-thirties. According to Leah Lovell (writing in the April 1995 issue of *International Writers Magazine*), "While in her parents' home, Miss Potter lived in the nursery, where she developed a love of studying the animals she found in hedgerows, such as rabbits, hedgehogs, squirrels, and frogs." She did watercolor paintings of the animals and made up stories about them. In 1900 her book about the mischievous Peter Rabbit was published, and she later became engaged to Peter Warne, the son of her publisher. He died before they could be married, and she moved to a farm in the

GO TO NEXT PAGE

Language Arts

north country. Even though she continued writing and painting, she also became known for her knowledge of farming and sheepbreeding. She married William Heelis, who was a solicitor, and the two lived on herfarm for the rest of their lives.Upon her death, she bequeathed her land to the National Trust of England. Her hundreds of watercolor paintings hang in museums and in private collections. Her children's books are still

Step 1

Determine when to use sources.

1. **When is it necessary to use sources for writing reports or speeches?**

_____

_____

2. **Is the subject of this report familiar enough for the writer to have had enough knowledge to write a report?**

_____

_____

Step 2

As you write, be sure to use your own words to present the material.

3. **Are the facts in the report in the same order as the facts in the magazine article?**

_____

4. **How else can you tell that the writer used his or her own words to write the report?**

_____

_____

Step 3

Indicate information that has been picked up from a source.

5. **Which sentence in the report was picked up from the magazine article?**

_____

_____

_____

6. **How did the writer of the report let readers know that this sentence was a quotation?**

_____

_____

**Open-Ended
Question**

7. Think about your answer to the following question. Write your answer on the lines. Be prepared to talk about your answer in a classroom discussion. From what you know about the Peter Rabbit stories and other Beatrix Potter stories, why do you think they have been so popular with children?

_____

_____

**Ideas to
Remember**

> **source**–a printed book or magazine that contains information about a topic

**Guided
Practice
Activity**

Your assignment is to write a report about the history of amusement parks in the United States.

8. **What kinds of sources would you need to use in order to complete your research on this topic?**

_____

_____

_____

9. **Why should you not use word-for-word a whole paragraph from one of your sources?**

_____

_____

10. **What parts of your sources is it legal to use? How must they be written?**

_____

_____

11. **Would it be all right to include a one-sentence quote by a famous author who has written a book on this topic?**

_____

12. **How should any quotations be presented so that the readers of your report know that they are quotations and not your own words?**

_____

_____

**Application
Activity**

Read the paragraphs below. Then answer the questions that follow.

The currency—coins and paper money—of the United States is made in factories known as mints, all under the direction of the Bureau of Engraving and Printing. Workers fill many different kinds of jobs at mints. One job is to replace damaged currency. Some currency, particularly paper money, is pulled out of circulation when it is badly

GO TO NEXT PAGE

Language Arts

damaged or worn. Currency that has been mutilated—burned, torn, or partially decomposed can be turned in to a mint, and it will be replaced if fifty-one percent of the bill can be patched together. People who lose cash in fires often take ashes to a mint in order to have the cash they lost replaced. Actually, money is hard to destroy. Paper money is made from paper that is three-fourths cotton fiber and one-fourth linen fiber. Blue and red fibers are added for identification. The paper is very durable and can be identified even after it has been burned.

When a specific denomination is designed, engravers use antique tools called "gravers" to engrave, or cut, the design into quarter-inch-thick steel plates. Every design is made up of lines, dots, and dashes that are cut into the steel plates by hand. When the engraving is finished, the plates are used to put ink onto the paper. Four of the engraved plates are fastened to a drum that spins. The printing process has three steps. In the first, the plates are smeared with the gooey, hot ink. In the second step, the surface of the plates is wiped clean, leaving ink in the grooves cut by the engravers. In the third step, the paper is squeezed against the plates. The pressure created by the squeezing process is twenty-five tons of weight per square inch. The ink remains on the paper, forming mounds. Often, people who read braille can tell the denomination of paper money by feeling the mounds on the paper.

13. **What would be the topic of a report using these two paragraphs as sources? Circle the letter of your answer.**
    a. how to counterfeit money
    b. how money is made
    c. how to redeem damaged money

14. **What can you use from these paragraphs and still avoid copying? Circle the letter of your answer.**
    a. an entire paragraph
    b. only the first sentence of each paragraph
    c. facts, details, and short quotations

15. **What must you do when you quote information from a source? Circle the letter of your answer.**
    a. use quotation marks and cite the source
    b. identify the source and pay the author
    c. put the line in boldface type

16. **Imagine that you are using the two paragraphs as a source for a report. Rewrite the information in your own words. Write your own paragraph on the lines below. Use one line from the paragraphs as a quote.**

_____

_____

_____

_____

Open-Ended Question

17. **Use a separate piece of paper or write in your literary response journal. Refer to the information in the Application Activity.**

    People who counterfeit money now use copy machines to duplicate currency.

    ● How would paper put through a copy machine compare to real money?

    ● How do you think people are able to identify counterfeit money and catch the counterfeiters?

Extension Activities

Reading Prompt ● Examining Book Reviews

Individual Activity

18. **Skim book reviews that appear in magazines such as *Time* and *Newsweek* or in your local daily paper. Have the reviewers quoted the books they are reviewing? Have they quoted other reviewers? Determine which reviews have used quotes and how the sources were cited. Share your information with the group.**

_____

_____

_____

_____

Writing Prompt ● Writing a Book Report

Cooperative Group Activity

19. **Work with a group. Have each member of the group read a book and write a report on it. Be sure to include basic ideas and concepts from the book but written in your own words. Make sure that you cite any quotes used from the book and identify the source appropriately in your report. Share your reports among the group.**

_____

_____

_____

Speaking Prompt ● Using Technology to Research Professional Standards

Workplace Readiness Activity

20. **Work with a group. Use electronic sources or library sources to determine how professionals such as doctors and other scientists cite the sources of their research. Find out how they present their sources when they present papers to professional meetings. Determine what standards each profession adheres to. Present your findings and samples to the class.**

_____

_____

_____

Sharing: Consideration of Audience and Selecting Media Forms and Types of Presentation

Classroom Discussion

What are the different kinds of media? Which ones do most people come in contact with on a daily basis? How do the media affect modern life?

Classroom Activity

Read the following paragraph. Then answer the questions in the boxes.

One of the most popular Tejana singers of all time was Selena Quintanilla. This amazing woman began her career as a small child performing in a family band. Her brother played guitar, while her sister played drums. Other musicians were hired as the years passed. Selena's Spanish-language songs were hits in Latin America, especially in Mexico, where hundreds of thousands of albums were sold. Selena's last album was done in English.

Step 1

Choose the appropriate audience for this material.

1. **Who is the topic of this material?**

   _____

2. **What is the main idea about the material?**

   _____

   _____

3. **What audience would probably be most interested in the information presented here?**

   _____

4. **Would this report be of interest to a general audience? Explain.**

   _____

   _____

   _____

GO TO NEXT PAGE

Step 2

Choose the best
media form for
this material.

5. **Which of the following media forms would this report fit into best? On the lines explain your answer.**
   a. Internet
   c. speech
   b. pamphlet
   d. letter

   _____

   _____

   _____

6. **What kind of Internet sites would be best for posting this report as an e-mail?**

   _____

7. **What audience could you reach if you presented this report as a letter?**

   _____

   _____

Step 3

Choose the
presentation that
would be best for
this material.

8. **Is this material fiction or nonfiction?**

   _____

9. **Would a written form or an oral form be the best presentation, or does it matter in what form this material is presented?**

   _____

   _____

10. **Which of the media forms might you use in presenting this information?**
    a. photos
    c. maps
    b. cassettes or CDs
    d. graphs

11. **Explain why you chose the type of presentation you did.**

   _____

   _____

   _____

 Language Arts

Open-Ended Question

12. Think about your answer to this question. Write your answer on the lines. Be prepared to talk about your answer in a classroom discussion. Why is it important to check out printed sources of information you encounter on television, on the radio, or on the Internet?

_____

_____

_____

_____

_____

_____

_____

_____

_____

Ideas to Remember

audience–the people you want to reach with your information

media–the various outlets for information, including television, radio, movies, print, the Internet, etc.

Guided Practice Activity

Read the notes for the next section of material about Selena. Answer the questions that follow.

"Selena and Los Dinos" won many awards for their work.

Three radio stations named Selena their female vocalist of the year in 1986 and 1987.

Of four nominations, Selena won female vocalist of the year once for the West Texas Hispanic Music Awards in 1987.

The Mike Chavez Awards of 1987 gave the group six nominations, and Selena won female vocalist of the year. She was only one of two women to win any of the 21 Mike Chavez awards handed out.

She or the band were nominated for 36 Tejano Music Awards, and they won 19 of these awards. She won female vocalist for the years 1986, 1987 and 1989–1995. She was performer of the year in 1986 and female entertainer of the year 1990–1995. She won album of the year from 1993–1995. In 1995 she also won record of the year and her song "Bidi Bidi Bom Bom" won song of the year.

For 1993, Selena won female vocalist of the year at the Cable ACE Awards in New York.

Her top award came in 1995, when she won a Grammy in Los Angeles for best Mexican American album for *Selena Live*.

13. What audience would probably be most interested in the information presented here?

_____

_____

_____

14. Would this report be of interest to a general audience? Explain.

_____

_____

_____

15. Which of the following media forms would this report fit into best? On the lines explain your answer.

a. Internet   c. speech

b. pamphlet   d. letter

_____

_____

16. What kind of Internet sites would be best for posting this report as an e-mail?

_____

_____

_____

17. Would a written form or an oral form be the best presentation, or does it matter what form in which this material is presented?

_____

_____

_____

18. Why would it be useful to play cassettes or CDs in presenting this information?

_____

_____

_____

19. Explain why you chose the type of presentation you did.

_____

_____

_____

          Language Arts

**Application
Activity**

**Use the following facts to create a conclusion for the material about Selena. Explain how you
would present this material and the kinds of media forms and the type of presentation you
would choose.**

also interested in fashion and jewelry

designed many of her own costumes

designed costumes for the band, too

dreamed of selling designs

opened her first boutique, Selena Etc., in 1994

became a chain, managed by president of her fan club

recorded her first English-language album (1995)

expected by top record executives to become a world-wide hit

Yolanda Saldovar, the manager of her stores, stole money

held a private meeting with Yolanda

shot and killed Selena at meeting on March 31, 1995

funeral watched by millions of fans around the world

20. Conclusion:

_____

_____

_____

_____

_____

_____

_____

21. Kinds of Media Forms:

_____

_____

_____

22. Type of Presentation:

_____

_____

_____

Open-Ended Question

23. Use a separate piece of paper or write in your literary response journal. Refer to the information in this lesson.

   - Who is your favorite singer, and what is your favorite style of music?

   - What qualities make you appreciate this entertainer and the entertainer's work?

Extension Activities

Viewing Prompt ● Analyzing Illustrations

Individual Activity

24. **Look through books from the library or media center for illustrations of people involved in some event. Do not read the material that accompanies the illustration, but examine the illustration. What are the people doing? How do they seem to be affected by the situation? Do the people seem to have some sort of goal? What are they trying to achieve? Jot down your ideas about the content of the illustration. Now, examine the information that accompanies the illustration. How well do your notes match the actual events? Why are illustrations effective items to include in a report or a speech?**

Writing Prompt ● Choosing an Audience and Form of Presentation

Cooperative Group Activity

25. **Work with a small group. List some topics for possible reports or speeches. Where would you find information on this topic? What kinds of details would be presented for each one? Who would most enjoy or benefit from a presentation of this topic? How would you present each set of material? Create a chart that lists the topics, the audience for each one, and the kind of presentation that could be made. Share your chart with those completed by other groups in your class.**

Speaking Prompt ● Setting Goals

Workplace Readiness Activity

26. **Work with a group. Discuss the kinds of careers that interest the members of the group. What kinds of skills are required for each job? Do the jobs require college educations? What high school classes will enable you to enter a college program for the jobs you desire? What extra-curricular activities will help make each student a more attractive applicant for colleges and universities? Create a group speech about the careers you examine and research. Create posters, videos, tapes, and other forms of media which will help you make your presentation. Work with other groups from the class to present your speeches for the class or to the school. Which speeches were the most effective? What qualities enhanced these speeches?**

                     Language Arts

Publishing and Public Speaking:
Preparing for and Making the Presentation

Classroom Discussion

Why is preparation so important in any endeavor that you attempt? How does practice produce better athletes, musicians, and actors? Why is practice important in developing the skills you need in order to succeed in school?

Classroom Activity

Read and examine the information below. Answer the questions that follow.

What must you do to prepare for a presentation of the material you have gathered for a report, an essay, a speech, or other ways of presenting information?

Step 1

Proofreading carefully is the key to well-prepared material.

1. **What is the purpose for proofreading?**
   _____

2. **Why should you learn to pronounce all the words you will be using in a speech?**
   _____
   _____

3. **Why must note cards for a speech be neatly prepared?**
   _____
   _____

4. **Why should your note cards include prompts on about media you plan to use?**
   _____

5. **Why should reports and other written material be neatly prepared?**
   _____
   _____

6. **How will punctuation, grammar, and spelling mistakes affect your written material?**
   _____

7. **How will accurately citing and punctuating your sources affect your written material?**
   _____
   _____

Step 2

Carefully check the media that will be a part of your presentation.

8. How will improperly prepared media affect a presentation?

_____

9. Why should posters, graphics, charts, and maps be neatly prepared?

_____

_____

10. What will happen to your presentation if you fail to make sure that projectors and tape or CD players are working properly and are set at a comfortable volume?

_____

_____

Step 3

Practice your presentation.

11. Why is practice important in making a presentation?

_____

_____

12. Why should you practice speaking clearly and carefully?

_____

13. Why should you practice to find a comfortable rhythm to use when speaking?

_____

_____

14. How will a thorough knowledge of your material help you during a question-and-answer period?

_____

_____

Open-Ended Question

15. Think about your answers to the following questions. Write your answers on the lines. Be prepared to talk about your answers in a classroom discussion. Will these steps be useful in helping people lessen their fears of presenting material in public? Why or why not?

_____

_____

_____

_____

90 Language Arts

Ideas to Remember

oral presentation–a talk or speech given to an audience

publish–to print a written report of a story so that it is available to others

Guided Practice Activity

How will you actually present your report or your speech? Read the steps and answer the questions.

Step 1

Consider the audience for your presentation.

16. Your report describes the benefits of using organic techniques instead of chemical fertilizers and insecticides. Who would be the best audience for this report?

_____

_____

17. Your speech is about the history of the space program. Who would be the best audience for your speech?

_____

_____

Step 2

Decide what form you will use for your writing.

As you prepare written material, you might be creating a **report**, a **theme**, a **booklet**, or other written materials. In these materials you might include drawings, maps, photographs, and other types of graphic illustrations. Presenting a poster can enhance your work and pique your audience's interest in your central idea and supporting details. You might even decide to use the **Internet** and include this information for your own web site or a site maintained by your school or school district.

18. What form would be appropriate for material concerning organic techniques of gardening?

_____

_____

_____

19. What form should you use for a paper that describes the history of the space program?

_____

_____

_____

Step 3

Decide how you
can make your
presentation easily
available to
your audience.

20. Which would be the best form and place for a presentation concerning the benefits of organic techniques of gardening? Circle your answer.

a. as a poster displayed in the gymnasium

b. as a poster displayed in a science class

c. as a booklet stored in the local library

Application
Activity

Read the paragraphs from a report or speech. Think about the ways of preparing and then presenting this material. Then answer the questions that follow.

Have you ever heard of the mysterious lemming? This animal looks something like a mouse and lives in Scandinavia, the cold region of northeastern Europe. They hibernate, or sleep, over the winter, and survive by living off the fat they have stored in their bodies during the warm months of spring and summer. To remain safe during hibernation, lemmings dig burrows, or tunnels, deep in the ground. There they do not freeze and can sleep undisturbed.

With spring, lemmings awake and move out of their burrows. In the spring, they look like they are almost starved, which, in reality, they are. They have used up all the body fat. The lemmings spend the warm months eating such foods as roots and moss. These animals eat as much as they can so that they can replenish the layers of fat they will need again for the next winter. Babies are born during hibernation, so that they can fatten themselves during the spring, too.

From time to time, the numbers of lemmings grow so huge that the land cannot support them. There is not enough food for all the lemmings to prepare for winter. That is when the mystery of the lemmings takes place. Thousands upon thousands begin a march to the sea, but some do remain behind. They devour every plant in their paths, including crops. The destruction points the direction in which the lemmings are headed. They do not stop at the shore but stumble over each other in the rush to enter the sea. They do not swim well, but can float for a long time. When the lemmings tire, they drown. Those lemmings who have remained behind fatten themselves for the winter, so the cycle begins again. No one knows why lemmings commit mass suicide in this way, how the lemmings decide who is to survive, or even how they know when their numbers have become so great that the species' very existence is threatened. This is a mystery that will puzzle scientists for years to come.

21. What book in the library is a source for the pronunciations and spellings of unfamiliar words? Circle your answer.

a. a thesaurus

b. a dictionary

c. an encyclopedia

 Language Arts

22. What book is the best source for rules to follow in checking grammar and punctuation?

a. an English textbook

b. a dictionary

c. a thesaurus

23. What type of printed material is the best source to use in making sure that the facts in this paragraph are correct?

a. magazines and newspapers

b. web sites on the Internet

c. an encyclopedia

24. Which paragraph would be enhanced by showing the audience a map of the world?

a. Paragraph 1

b. Paragraph 2

c. Paragraph 3

25. Which paragraph would be enhanced with a diagram of animal habitats?

a. Paragraph 3

b. Paragraph 2

c. Paragraph 1

26. Which paragraph would be enhanced with a film or video that shows live action?

a. Paragraph 3

b. Paragraph 2

c. Paragraph 1

27. How would practicing this material in the room where it was to be presented as a speech be helpful?

_____

_____

_____

_____

Open-Ended Question

28. Use a separate piece of paper or write in your literary response journal. Refer to the information in this lesson.

● Do you agree or disagree with the idea that all animal behavior results from instinct rather than learning?

● How do you think geography and climate affect the behaviors of animals?

Extension Activities

Speaking Prompt ● Practicing a Presentation

Individual Activity

29. **Choose a short selection from one of your textbooks to practice as if it were a speech. How will you familiarize yourself with this material? What sources can you check to make sure that you understand the material and how it should be presented? Practice giving the speech in front of a mirror. How much practice did you need before you felt comfortably prepared? Share your experience with the class.**

_____

_____

_____

_____

_____

Speaking Prompt ● Examining Presentation Techniques

Cooperative Group Activity

30. **Work with a group. Discuss the ideas presented in this lesson. Which ones will be the most time consuming? For which techniques do the members feel they need to strengthen their skills? How would a checklist help a speaker ensure the success of a speech? What items should be part of this checklist? Work with the other groups form the class in preparing a checklist.**

_____

_____

_____

_____

_____

Listening Prompt ● Conducting an Interview

Workplace Readiness Activity

31. **Work with a group. Invite speakers to conduct a career day for your class or the school. Talk about the kinds of things you wish to learn from these people? Why is it just as important for an audience to prepare for a presentation as it is for a speaker? What steps will you take in preparing for the career day? How will a list of questions help you achieve your goals for this day? If possible, different groups could conduct videotaped interviews with the speakers after the main presentation is complete.**

_____

_____

_____

_____

_____

 Language Arts

Multiple Choice
Read the following questions and the four possible answers. Choose the answer to each question. Find the bubble next to the question that has the same letter as the answer you chose. Fill in this bubble to mark your answer.

Ⓐ Ⓑ Ⓒ Ⓓ 1. **What kinds of details are included in written materials or speeches that inform?**
a. fantasy   c. fiction
b. opinions   d. facts

Ⓐ Ⓑ Ⓒ Ⓓ 2. **If a report or speech tries to convince an audience to accept an idea or suggestion, what is its purpose?**
a. instruct   c. entertain
b. persuade   d. give directions

Ⓐ Ⓑ Ⓒ Ⓓ 3. **Which technique is the best one to use for organizing facts and ideas in order of importance?**
a. outlining   c. finding a source
b. finding a topic   d. plagiarizing

Ⓐ Ⓑ Ⓒ Ⓓ 4. **What type of literature is presented as plays?**
a. nonfiction   c. poetry
b. drama   d. word pictures

Ⓐ Ⓑ Ⓒ Ⓓ 5. **What are opinions?**
a. a person's beliefs   c. a person's central ideas
b. a person's ideas that can be proven d. a person's topics

Ⓐ Ⓑ Ⓒ Ⓓ 6. **Which of the following terms describes the author's opinion or feelings about a topic or subject?**
a. closing   c. main idea
b. point of view   d. opening

Ⓐ Ⓑ Ⓒ Ⓓ 7. **What literary device compares two things using the words "like" or "as"?**
a. metaphor   c. simile
b. foreshadowing   d. symbol

Ⓐ Ⓑ Ⓒ Ⓓ 8. **What literary device is also an example of personification?**
a. foreshadowing   c. symbol
b. metaphor   d. simile

Ⓐ Ⓑ Ⓒ Ⓓ 9. **What are all the different ways of presenting information?**
a. audience   c. figures of speech
b. performance   d. media

Ⓐ Ⓑ Ⓒ Ⓓ 10. **Which word describes making a written report or story available to others in print?**
a. present   c. edit
b. publish   d. speak in public

Writing Prompt ● My Fantasy Vacation

Situation

You have been granted three wishes so that your fantasy vacation will come true. How will you use these wishes?

Before You Write

What are the techniques for presenting written material? Think about the following ideas:

- What purpose do you want to accomplish—entertain, inform, persuade, instruct, or give directions?

- What will be the topic of your writing?

- Which literary forms might help you achieve this purpose?

- Where in all the world would you most like to go?

- How would you like to spend your time at this place?

- How can you state these goals as three wishes?

- Why will these actions make you happy?

- How will you choose, organize, and sequence the ideas to be presented in your writing?

- What audience do you want to reach?

- What special materials would help you present your ideas?

Write a description of your fantasy vacation and how you will use your three wishes to make it come true. Be sure to write your topic, main idea or theme, supporting details, opinions, and conclusions simply and clearly. Complete your work on a separate piece of paper. You may wish to write in your literary response journal instead.

Speaking Prompt ● Winning the Olympics

Situation

You have just won a gold medal at the latest Olympic games. What are your reactions to this achievement?

Before You Speak

How can you convey these feelings to your audience? Think about the following ideas:

- What will be the topic of your speech?

- What Olympic event will be part of the central idea of your speech?

- How do these games present medals to winners?

- How have winners of past games that you have seen seemed to react to winning gold medals?

- Why would a person experience many kinds of feelings upon achieving such a lofty goal?

- How can literary devices help you convey your feelings in a speech?

- What media will you use to present your speech?

Present a short speech explaining how you feel about winning a gold medal at the latest Olympic games. Prepare your ideas on a separate piece of paper. Be sure to include a topic, main idea or theme, supporting details, opinions, and conclusions. You can use such things as pictures, photographs, charts, diagrams, and note cards in your presentation. Speak clearly and confidently as you make your speech.

Language Arts

Introduction

Classroom Discussion

Have you ever prepared food with a mix? How did you know what to do? If you get a new board game, how do you know how to play it?

Classroom Activity

Look at the picture below. Answer the questions that follow.

1. **Which of these pictures show information sources that require listening?**

_____

2. **Which of these pictures show information sources that require reading?**

_____

3. **Which of these pictures show information sources that require both reading and listening?**

_____

4. **Which of these information sources can be read or listened to for pleasure?**

_____

5. **Which of these sources can be read or listened to for useful information?**

_____

 97

Classroom Discussion

As you read or listen to learn, how do you remember the main points that an author or speaker is making? How do you determine what is important to remember and what is not?

Classroom Activity

To understand what you are reading, or to understand what a speaker intends by a speech, you must first identify the topic about which you are reading or listening. Next, you must identify central ideas, and then supporting details. If you can identify all these, then you will understand the main points of what you are reading or hearing.

Read and examine the information below. Then answer the questions that follow.

As you eat, do you ever wonder who made the dishes you are eating from or how they were made? Some dishes are mass produced and are not expensive, but others are made by hand and can cost thousands of dollars. Expensive dishes are usually china, and much of it is made as individual pieces. One city in England, Stoke-on-Trent, is known as "The Potteries" because it is composed of six small towns that each specialize in making a particular kind of china.

China is made from a mixture of clay called kaolin, china stone known as petuntse, and bone. Both kaolin and petuntse are decomposed granite, but kaolin is further decomposed than petuntse. It is very white and slippery. The petuntse is rougher in texture. The bone is from oxen and cattle, and it is ground almost to ash before it is added to the mixture. Bone gives the china strength and makes it translucent. Potters in Stoke use kaolin and petuntse from Cornwall. The pottery makers originally moved to Stoke for the pure clay and stone, for coal to burn in the kilns, and for lead and salt to glaze the pottery.

Years ago, making pottery could be deadly. The china is fired to harden each piece and set the glaze, and people who worked in the older factories constantly breathed the smoke from the kilns. Many of the designs that were painted on the pottery contained arsenic, which is a poison. Lead was used in the glazing process, and so lead poisoning was always a danger. Potters often became sick with a disease known as "potter's rot," which is a crippling lung disease. Workers who put the china in the kiln to be fired and then removed it usually had their eyebrows and eyelashes singed off from the tremendous heat, and many suffered the symptoms of dehydration.

China factories today are very different from the factories of eighty years ago. Pieces of pottery are rarely thrown on a wheel by hand anymore. Potters now pour the liquid clay mixture into plaster-of-paris molds. A machine called the "jolly" is used for forming bowls, cups, and tureens. Kilns used for setting and glazing are now heated with electricity or gas, doing away with coal smoke. Pieces that are in the kiln for drying or glazing are placed on a trolley that is moved automatically through the kiln, so no one goes in and out of the kiln's vicious heat. Since arsenic and lead are no longer used in the china-making process, workers are no longer in danger of being poisoned by their work.

GO TO NEXT PAGE

When china is made today, the first step is either pouring the liquid clay mixture, or slip, into molds or molding the thick clay with either a jolly or a plate mold. The molded forms are then put on a trolley and moved through the kiln to be dried. After drying, the pieces are known as "biscuit." The next step is decoration. Some decoration is applied before glazing and some is applied after. Transfers are applied before glazing. Once a transfer is applied, the piece is put back into the kiln to set the color and burn off any oil from the transfer. If colors are to be very bright and the design is to be painted instead of transferred, the glaze is applied first, and then the pieces are decorated. Pieces are dipped into the glaze, which is like liquid glass made from ground clay and flint mixed with water. After the glaze is applied, the pieces are put into the kiln again for about thirty hours. If colors are to be applied in layers, the piece may be fired after each color application. If gold, or gilt, is applied to china, it is fired, scoured with fine silver sand, and then burnished. Many steps go into the creation of every piece of fine china.

Wedgewood, Minton, Doulton, Royal Crown Derby, and Mason's china are all made in Stoke-on-Trent, as are many other brands. The town of Coalport specializes in china flowers. Mason's china has two specialties—one is deep, rich colors and oriental patterns, and the other is pottery so strong it can be made into garden seats and beds. Some of Doulton's china is famous for the sculpting on it. Doulton has even set up a school to train sculptors, who, upon finishing, may or may not work for Doulton. Minton specializes in strong colors, but much of its requested work is for hand-painted reproductions of photographs sent in by clients. Spode produces memorial services, such as a series on the War of 1812 to be sold in the United States. So, when you sit down to your next meal off a china plate, look at the plate carefully. It has undergone a long process to be produced, and it may have a story behind the pattern.

Step 1

Determine the topic of the reading selection or speech.

1. What is the topic of this selection?

_____

2. Why could you not use the topic "Dishes"?

_____

Step 2

As you read or listen, identify central ideas presented in the selection or speech.

3. What is the central idea of the third paragraph?

_____

_____

4. What is the central idea of the fifth paragraph?

_____

_____

Step 3

As you read or listen, identify supporting details for each central idea.

5. What are some supporting details in the third paragraph?

_____

_____

_____

_____

6. What are some supporting details in the fifth paragraph?

_____

_____

_____

_____

Open-Ended Question

7. Think about your answer to the following question. Write your answer on the lines. Be prepared to talk about your answer in a classroom discussion. Many people consider fine china to be as much a work of art as a practical item. Why do so many people still use it to serve food?

_____

_____

_____

_____

_____

_____

_____

_____

Ideas to Remember

topic–the person, place, thing, or idea that a writer or speaker is discussing

central idea–the major idea that a writer or speaker is presenting

supporting details–details that add to or support the central idea

Language Arts

Lesson 1   Recognition of Topic, Central Idea or Theme, and Supporting Details

Guided Practice Activity

Read the following information and answer the questions in the boxes.

Have you seen the animated movie or the Broadway production of *The Lion King*? If you have, you are familiar with an animal named Timon, who is a meerkat. Meerkats are not cats; they are close relatives of the mongoose, which is the inspiration for Rudyard Kipling's character Rikki-Tikki-Tavi. Meerkats live in colonies, and they divide the labor of the colony among themselves. Because they are small animals, they must watch for predators while they forage for food. Meerkats take turns being sentry and watching while the other animals hunt and eat. One of the females is selected or volunteers to be the nanny and watch the young while the other animals hunt for food. Those who must watch or babysit are brought food by the other animals. When enemies approach, meerkats band together and attack like a tiny army. Meerkat colonies are some of the most socially advanced groups of animals on Earth.

The meerkat is a small, slender animal with a triangular head. Its pointed snout makes its entire body seem pointed. It has a long stiff tail, which it uses as a prop to stand on its back legs and survey the surrounding area. Whiskers protrude from its pointed snout and sharp teeth can be seen from under its upper lip. The meerkat's front paws sport long, curved claws. Though its fur is thick and bushy, most of the time it looks sleek.

A meerkat usually will dart into its hole when an enemy approaches, but if the enemy surprises a group of meerkats, they will ban together and rush the animal. They fluff out their fur so that they resemble one big animal, and they rush in a wave toward the intruder. As they run, they emit a hissing growl that rises and falls. Most enemies consider this hissing, growling mob action something to be feared, and they run for their lives. Feeling they are succeeding in their attack, the meerkats give chase until the enemy is gone. After the tiny animals are safe, they begin patting, hugging, greeting, and grooming each other as if in congratulations for their bravery. While meerkats stay clear of large predators, they go out of their way to torment smaller, less threatening animals. Their behavior seems designed to warn smaller animals to stay out of their territory.

During a single day, meerkats have two objectives. The first is to find food, and the second is to watch for approaching predators. As they move from place to place, meerkats constantly search for food, pawing the ground, poking under and into bushes, and turning over rocks. They eat scorpions and insects, such as beetles and beetle grubs. At the first indication that a hole in the ground might harbor food, a meerkat will begin scratching and clawing to find it. Meerkats dig deep holes very quickly, and are so fast that they usually catch the prey they are seeking.

When two colonies of meerkats find each other, a standoff occurs. Both groups jump high into the air, always landing in the same place. Each group seems to want to scare the other with their energy. After bounding in place for a while, each group will begin to dig, throwing large clumps of soil into the air as if to demonstrate their power. After this display, both groups will rush toward each other. Usually one group will then break ranks and run away, abandoning the few stragglers, who get pummeled in a demonstration that the winning group will not tolerate such action. After the test of strength is completed and won, the winners go through their own kind of congratulatory ceremony, again hugging, patting, and grooming each other.

When babies are born, the females of the meerkat colony take turns baby-sitting while the mother searches for food. When it is time for the babies to go outside and begin learning the ways of the colony, they are protected by all its members. Each baby attaches itself to an adult, whether the adult happens to be its parent or not, and it is fed and taught by the adult.

Once night falls and the meerkats go back into their communal den, they curl up in one big, furry knot and go to sleep. Each member of the community is as important as every other member, and no single meerkat seems dominant.

Step 1

Determine the topic of the reading selection or speech.

8. What is the topic of this selection?

_____

Step 2

As you read or listen, identify central ideas presented in the selection or speech.

9. What is the central idea of the third paragraph ?

_____

_____

10. What is the central idea of the fifth paragraph?

_____

_____

Step 3

As you read or listen, identify supporting details for each central idea.

11. What are some supporting details in the third paragraph?

_____

_____

_____

_____

12. What are some supporting details in the fifth paragraph?

_____

_____

_____

_____

_____

                                  Language Arts

Application Activity

Read the information below. Then answer the questions that follow.

Helping Hands is an organization that trains capuchin monkeys. Why the name "Helping Hands"? Trainers in the organization teach the tiny monkeys to help people who have suffered severe spinal cord injuries and are paralyzed. The little monkeys bring food and drinks to their owners. They help in other ways, such as dialing phones, turning lights on or off, putting tapes in players, fetching whatever the owner wants, turning book pages, turning on computers, changing television channels, and even feeding their owners and combing or brushing their hair.

People who have severe spinal cord injuries have often lost all feeling and movement in their arms and legs, and they are completely dependent on others for everything, even a drink of water. Because it is very expensive to hire people to stay with a person who is confined to a wheelchair, it is much more cost effective to provide the person with a little monkey who can help with everything except getting the person in and out of bed or in and out of the wheelchair. The assistance provided by the monkeys makes injury patients more independent than they would be if they had to rely on other people all the time. Besides helping their owners, the capuchin monkeys provide them with entertainment by playing with other pets in the owner's home, romping around the owner's room, and engaging in other antics associated with monkeys.

Before settling on capuchin monkeys, Helping Hands tried working with chimpanzees. However, a grown chimp can be as large as a person and much stronger. It can also be grumpy and not want to cooperate. Capuchin monkeys, otherwise known as "organ-grinder" monkeys, are about eighteen inches tall when fully grown, and they rarely weigh more than five or six pounds. They also have better temperaments than chimps. Capuchins are very smart and easy to train. After training, they usually figure some things out for themselves. For instance, one monkey was being trained to drop an object into a tube in order to receive a treat. As the object touched the bottom of the tube, the treat was dispensed automatically. After a brief absence from the room, the trainer returned to find the treat bottle nearly empty. The monkey had been sticking the corner of its bedsheet into the tube to dispense a treat and had drunk up almost all of the sweet liquid in the treat bottle. Another capuchin tried to train its owner. When it would do something to help the owner, the owner was supposed to blow into a tube near her face to dispense a treat for the monkey. If she did not reward the monkey immediately, the little capuchin would push the owner's face near the tube so that the treat could be dispensed.

Capuchins sleep and live in big cages in the homes of their paralyzed owners. If a capuchin does something it's not supposed to do, its owner will send it to its cage. The monkey is trained to enter the cage and close the door until the owner says it is all right for it to be out in the room again.

Injury patients who have capuchins as their helpers find that they are no longer cut off from other people. Most people found that after their accidents, other people did not stop to talk to them if they were outside their homes. Accompanied by a small monkey, the owners find that many people stop to ask questions and talk about the assistance that the monkey gives to the owner. The monkeys love their owners and pet and touch them as if they were beloved family members. Most people who have capuchin monkeys to assist them say that not only are the monkeys helpful and reliable, they enrich the lives of their owners with love and attention.

GO TO NEXT PAGE

13. What is the topic of this article? Circle the letter of your answer.

a. capuchin monkeys and how they help people who are paralyzed

b. why capuchin moneys make good pets

c. how to reward monkeys for good behavior

14. What is the central idea of the third paragraph? Circle the letter of your answer.

a. Chimpanzees are dangerous animals with bad temperaments.

b. Adult chimpanzees grow to be as large as humans, and they weigh as much.

c. Capuchins were chosen over chimpanzees because of their size and temperament.

15. What is the central idea of the fourth paragraph? Circle the letter of your answer.

a. Capuchin monkeys hate living in cages.

b. Capuchin monkeys live in big cages in their owners' homes.

c. Capuchin monkeys always close the door when they go into their cages.

16. What is one supporting detail in the third paragraph? Circle the letter of your answer.

a. An adult capuchin monkey is about eighteen inches tall and weighs about five or six pounds.

b. One capuchin monkey drank all the liquid in its treat bottle.

c. One capuchin monkey reminds her owner when she should have a treat.

17. What is one supporting detail in the fourth paragraph? Circle the letter of your answer.

a. If monkeys do something they are not supposed to do, their owners send them to their cages.

b. A monkey that misbehaves must stay in its cage until its owner allows it to come out.

c. Capuchin monkeys sleep in their cages.

Open-Ended Question

18. Use a separate piece of paper or write in your literary response journal. Refer to the information in the Application Activity.

● Would it or would it not be worthwhile for trained monkeys to be provided free of charge for paralyzed people? Why?

● What are some other situations for which monkeys could be trained to help out humans?

Extension Activities

Writing Prompt ● **Evaluating Accomplishments**

Individual Activity

19. **Think back over your last school year. Think of your entire year as a central idea and your accomplishments as supporting details. Write a brief paragraph enumerating your accomplishments and then determine how successful you were last year in school.**

_____

_____

_____

_____

_____

Reading Prompt ● Identifying Central Ideas

Cooperative Group Activity

20. **Work with a group. Use your science textbook or your social studies or history textbook. Skim the chapter you are currently studying. Determine the central idea of each section in the chapter. Use these central ideas to formulate a study outline of the chapter.**

_____

_____

_____

_____

_____

Speaking Prompt ● Working Cooperatively with Others

Workplace Readiness Activity

21. **Work with a group. Use newspaper articles and television broadcasts to evaluate the local news for the past week. Identify the central ideas of each news story and include supporting details to finish out the stories. Present a news broadcast and commentary for the rest of the class that recaps and gives students' opinions about the local news of the past week.**

_____

_____

_____

_____

_____

**Classroom
Discussion**

As you follow directions, whether they are written or oral, how do you determine exactly what you must know or do to complete the task? What usually happens if you do not follow directions exactly?

**Classroom
Activity**

Details often are like clues that help you understand what you read or hear. Being able to select and use the most important clues can help you understand what you are hearing or reading.

Read and examine the information below. Then answer the questions that follow.

In the late 1800s and early 1900s, one woman attracted attention for a change in women's lifestyles. Her name was Annie Oakley, and she was a petite woman who starred in the Buffalo Bill Cody Wild West Show as a sharpshooter. While Susan B. Anthony, Elizabeth Cady Stanton, and other women were protesting the lack of rights for women and attempting to change laws so that women could vote, Annie Oakley was riding her horse around the ring of the wild west show shooting targets out of the air and off the heads of willing friends. In Annie Oakley, people saw a woman who used some of the major symbols of masculinity—shotguns, rifles, and pistols—better than any man could and still maintained her femininity. Annie Oakley showed the public that women could, indeed, excel in a man's world.

Before she became the fastest trick shot in the West, Annie Oakley was Phoebe Ann Moses. She was born in 1860 on a small farm in western Ohio. Her father died when she was five, leaving her mother in dire poverty. Phoebe Ann, at age eight, picked up her father's rifle and began hunting game to feed herself, her mother, and the other children in the family. The first time Phoebe Ann fired a shot the kick from the gun broke her nose; she and her brother had put too much powder in it. Phoebe Ann continued to hunt for food. Eventually, her mother had to place her with another farm family, who treated her badly. She was overworked and beaten. Her mother remarried, and Phoebe Ann moved back home, but she had to help her stepfather pay off a lien on their home. To do that, she hunted commercially and sold the game she killed to hotel dining rooms in Cincinnati. Phoebe Ann was already an accurate shot; the hotels paid extra because the game they bought from her was not riddled with buckshot.

Few people know very much about the performer Annie Oakley because, even though her public life was very public, she struggled to keep her private life private. She married another sharpshooter named Frank Butler one year after she beat him in a shooting contest. Frank went into show business as a sharpshooter, and Annie soon became his partner. They traveled from town to town showing off their talents with firearms until they were invited to join the Wild West show. The two worked well together, but Annie had a talent for acting and entertaining. She became the star, and Butler, now her husband, fell into the role of manager and coach. The two stayed with Buffalo Bill for seventeen seasons.

GO TO NEXT PAGE

Language Arts

One of the tricks that Annie Oakley became famous for was shooting the heart out of the center of an ace-of-hearts playing card. She could pick the center of the heart out so cleanly that tickets punched with hole punches are often referred to as "Annie Oakleys." She shot flames off of candles rotating on a wheel, she shot dimes out of men's hands, she shot backward by using a Bowie knife blade as a mirror, and she stood on a galloping horse and shot targets out of the air. She even did cartwheels and handsprings. Everyone loved the spunky little girl that Buffalo Bill Cody called "the maid of the West." Sitting Bull, who also toured with the Wild West show, called Annie "Little Sure Shot." At the height of her career, Annie made $1,000 a week, which was more than the President of the United States made.

When Annie and Frank retired to private life, they bought a home in Cambridge, Maryland, and settled in to enjoy the wildlife around their home. Later they moved to North Carolina, where Annie taught shooting to society women. During World War I, Annie came out of retirement briefly to entertain the soldiers. She appeared before audiences that eventually totaled half a million. After she broke a hip in an automobile accident, Annie became an invalid, and she moved back to Ohio, where she died. A few weeks after Annie's death, Frank Butler also died. A woman with an amazing career, Annie lived her life according to her own standards and died quietly years later, still by her own standards.

Step 1

Look for important details in what you read or hear.

1. **What is the topic of these paragraphs?**

   _____

2. **What kind of life did the main character live before she became famous?**

   _____

3. **What was Annie's career?**

   _____

4. **How did she get into this type of career?**

   _____

   _____

5. **What kind of life did Annie live offstage?**

   _____

Lesson 2

Step 2

Analyze details to interpret the ideas in what you read or hear.

6. **How did Annie Oakley learn to shoot?**

_____

7. **How did this bring about Annie's career?**

_____

_____

8. **How was her role different from other women who worked to gain equality for women?**

_____

_____

9. **Why did Annie want her private life to be private?**

_____

_____

Step 3

Identify the writer's or speaker's purpose by examining the details you found and the conclusions you have drawn.

10. **What is the purpose of these paragraphs? Circle the letter of the answer you choose.**
    a. The paragraphs were written to persuade readers that women should be given more rights.
    b. The paragraphs were written to inform readers about a performer who broke new ground for women.
    c. The paragraphs were written to instruct readers about what they should do to have a career in entertainment.

Open-Ended Question

11. Think about your answer to the following question. Write your answer on the lines. Be prepared to talk about your answer in a classroom discussion. Even though Annie Oakley made a great contribution to the cause of women's rights, she is still more widely known for being a sharpshooter. Why?

_____

_____

_____

_____

_____

_____

Ideas to Remember

topic–the person, place, thing, or idea that a writer or speaker is discussing

central idea–the major idea that a writer or speaker is presenting

detail–a fact or idea that tells more about a topic and the central idea about that topic

conclusion–an idea or opinion that can be formed based on the information in a piece of writing or in a speech

Guided Practice Activity

Read the following paragraphs. Then follow the steps and answer the questions.

Many heated debates over the passage of new laws and the abolishment of old ones take place in Congress today, both in the House of Representatives and in the Senate. However, none of the debates and arguments throughout the two hundred and thirty-plus years since the United States was founded have been as heated and bitter as the first great debate that created the document by which we operate the government of this country—the United States Constitution.

In the summer of 1787, a small group of men from the American confederation of states, gathered in the State House in Philadelphia, Pennsylvania. The men had been selected by the people in their respective states to write the Constitution. The summer air was sweltering hot, and so were the arguments and quarrels among the individuals who were attempting to work as a group to frame our government. One attempt had already been made to organize a government, using the Articles of Confederation, but because the Articles gave the government no real power, a replacement had to be drafted. Speeches went on for hours, and the debates lasted even longer. Alexander Hamilton, whose main interest was in having a strong central government, walked out of the convention at one point and declared that he would come back only if the rest of the group would assure him that it would not be a waste of his time. With the fight for independence from England just over, many of the delegates disagreed with Hamilton because they feared having a government like England's. The only reason that all the delegates continued meeting was that they were afraid of complete failure and what the people in their states would think and do if they failed. All the delegates understood that, in order to succeed, they would have to compromise with one another. George Washington reminded the group during one session that the world was watching them to determine whether democracy would really work, and if they did not settle disputes, the entire world would believe that people are incapable of governing themselves.

An even greater reason for the necessity of a unified government was that the thirteen states were threatened by other countries, even though they were independent. England was ready to try again to reestablish control over the states. France wanted repayment for the money it had loaned the colonies during the Revolution. Spain controlled Florida and was attempting to gain control of the western area of the continent by closing the Mississippi River to American trade. Settlers who did not want to live in the cities of the East had begun moving to the western area not yet claimed by the United States. All delegates to the Convention feared that if these people received support from other countries, they would form new countries intent on invading the United States. The delegates understood that the future of the United States rested on a time bomb that would eventually explode, with the possibility of destroying the country they had worked so hard to create.

The major fear of the Convention delegates was that the central government control they instituted would either be too much or too little. James Madison's idea was that any person with power should be distrusted, so he was not willing to put most of the power of government in the hands of one person. Other delegates, however, feared that if most of the power were put into the hands of the population as a whole, their various interests would cause different groups to go to war with each other. Smaller states feared what might happen to them if their larger neighbors were given more power than they. States that allowed enslavement feared that states that prohibited it would free the slaves. States that prohibited enslavement feared that states that allowed it would see to it that enslavement became a nationwide policy. James Madison kept the process moving by proposing what became known as the Virginia Plan.

The Virginia Plan allowed for three branches of government—judicial, executive, and legislative—with all members either to be elected or appointed. The plan also called for a bicameral, or two-housed, legislature. The next argument that stalled the Convention was how much power these two houses would have, how much power each state would have, and how the members of the two houses would be chosen to serve. Another fear also developed, which was whether individual states would still have their own governments, or whether the central government took over all powers. The group also could not settle on whether they wanted an extremely powerful President or whether the executive branch would be composed of a council. Madison assured the delegates that a single President could not take advantage of power if the legislative branch could veto executive actions. He also felt that democracy would work because people would have such wide interests that they would not be inclined to band together against other groups. The next argument concerned how members of the legislative branch would be selected. Many of the delegates felt that ordinary citizens were not informed enough to vote for people to represent them. The fear that larger states would hold more power over smaller states was overwhelming for many of the delegates.

Issue after issue arose, was debated, and finally decided upon. The Convention began on June 27. Debates continued until July 16, when a majority of the delegates agreed to what became known as The Great Compromise. Work continued on the document that would rule the United States until the United States Constitution was signed on September 17, 1787. After that time, the Bill of Rights was added. Even though it has been amended many times, the United States Constitution continues to be the document that sets the laws for this country and the people who live in it.

Step 1

Look for important details in what you read or hear.

12. Where and how was the United States Constitution written?

_____

_____

13. Why did these people serve as delegates to write the Constitution?

_____

_____

GO TO NEXT PAGE

14. What were some of the major points on which the delegates disagreed?

_____

_____

_____

_____

_____

Step 2

Analyze details to
interpret the ideas
in what you read
or hear.

15. Why were so many delegates fearful of a strong central government?

_____

_____

_____

_____

_____

16. Why was it absolutely necessary that the states unite to form a central government?

_____

_____

_____

_____

_____

17. Why were the delegates determined to reach some sort of agreement before they went back to their own states?

_____

_____

_____

_____

_____

Step 3

Identify the writer's or speaker's purpose by examining the details you found and the conclusions you have drawn.

Application Activity

18. What is the purpose of this paragraph? Circle the letter of your answer.
   a. The paragraphs were written to inform readers about how the Constitution was written.
   b. The paragraphs were written to show some of the entertaining incidents that happened when the Constitution was written.
   c. The paragraphs were written to instruct readers about how to write important legal documents.

Read the information below. Then answer the questions that follow.

Are you aware that scientists known as glaciologists have predicted weather trends by using ancient air? Where does the air come from? Glaciers! These huge sheets of ancient ice contain bubbles of air that have been encased in the ice for thousands of years. As snow fell and the ice built up, air was trapped and frozen into the glaciers. The air has remained intact and uncontaminated over the centuries. Tracing different gases present in the air bubbles allows scientists to track weather over thousands of years and to predict what the weather on Earth will be like over the next several centuries.

For years, scientists felt that if they could get samples of air that had been unchanged for thousands of years, they could determine what atmospheric conditions caused changes in weather patterns. The only trouble was that it was almost impossible to find ancient air that had not been contaminated with air from later periods. One group of scientists tried extracting ancient air from amber. Insects are trapped in tree sap that hardens into the gem amber, but air bubbles are also trapped. This group felt that if they could extract the air from the bubbles, they would have pure, uncontaminated ancient air. What they found, though, was that amber leaks air just like plastic, and that the air bubbles inside the amber had leaked some of their own gases to the outside and absorbed some of the outside air into the bubbles. We now know that the air bubbles inside amber are contaminated with modern air. Other scientists tried the air inside Egyptian pyramids, hourglasses, pocketwatches, and other items that contain air that has been sealed up for long periods. All have shown contamination of some sort—all except glacier ice.

Glaciologists use tubes attached to drill bits to drill down into glacier ice and take samples called "cores." Inside the cores are bubbles of air that were frozen into the ice when new snow fell and added a layer of ice to the glaciers. By cracking pieces of the core with a device that crushes the ice to bits, scientists free the air from centuries ago. The air is captured and then analyzed with a laser. Because weather can be determined from the past, glaciologists have determined how much carbon dioxide was present in Earth's atmosphere when the ice ages began, exactly when carbon dioxide levels began to change, and how much carbon dioxide was present in the atmosphere when the ice ages were ending and ice was retreating from the southern reaches of the northern hemisphere. By comparing ancient samples with our modern air, glaciologists have been able to determine that we are currently at the end of an ice age.

Scientists analyzing the air from glaciers have found that volcanic eruptions are marked by traces of sulfuric acid. The ancient ice also shows how human presence and activity affects the atmosphere and then the environment. The amount of lead present in the atmosphere 27,000 years ago has grown to 200

Language Arts

times that amount. The early lead came from sea spray, volcanic eruptions, and soil dust. The greater amount of lead in today's atmosphere comes from human activity. Falling snow and rain have also increased their acidity. However, the greatest increase is in carbon dioxide, and it increases constantly. This rapid increase can be attributed to the burning of fossil fuels. The amount of carbon dioxide decreases rapidly with an approaching ice age. When the weather warms back up after an ice age, the amount of carbon dioxide increases. It is the increases and decreases in carbon dioxide amounts that indicate what will happen to the weather. By measuring the amounts of other compounds present in the atmosphere over centuries, scientists have found that climate can "snap," or change suddenly. Sudden warm periods have occurred during ice ages, and in periods of warming the climate has suddenly cooled. Research is being conducted on whether the amounts of compounds that humans are putting into the atmosphere can cause the climate to snap, or whether changes that are indicated now are gradual but certain. Many scientists feel that we are causing the climate to become warmer and warmer—a trend known as "global warming." However, they are reluctant to predict what the changing trend will cause because we really have no way of knowing that. Most scientists who have used the ancient glacial air to predict global warming fear that if they begin predicting what will happen as a result, people will prepare for something that might not happen. They feel that the best plan for the future is to gather more information to reach a closer determination about the future of Earth and its climate.

19. Why is it important for scientists to know what Earth's climate has been like in the past? Circle the letter of your answer.

a. They can determine exactly when changes in Earth's climate have occurred in order to determine exactly when the dinosaurs died.

b. They can determine the exact conditions of an ice age in order to determine whether Earth is experiencing an ice age right now.

c. They can use climate trends to determine what changes might occur in the future climate in order to prepare for any extreme changes that might affect people's lives.

20. Why did using the air bubbles trapped in amber and other sources not work? Circle the letter of your answer.

a. Air bubbles trapped in amber and other sources are much more difficult to obtain and analyze than those trapped in ice.

b. Air bubbles trapped in amber and other sources have been found to have exchanged air with the outside, and are therefore contaminated.

c. Air bubbles trapped in amber and other sources were blown in by human breath, and so they are only carbon dioxide and are not good indicators.

21. What effect traced through the centuries has made climate unpredictable? Circle the letter of your answer.

a. the increase of acid in precipitation

b. snaps, or sudden changes in climate

c. the increased amount of lead in the atmosphere

22. Explain why the core samples taken from glaciers contain bubbles of ancient air that has not been contaminated.

_____

_____

Open-Ended Question

23. Use a separate piece of paper or write in your literary response journal. Refer to the information in the Application Activity.

- Why are scientists reluctant to predict what will happen in the future to the Earth's climate?

- What do you think would happen if dire predictions were made?

- What would happen if major predictions turned out to be wrong?

Extension Activities

Reading Prompt ● Extrapolating Information

Individual Activity

24. **Listen to news broadcasts for one evening. Take notes about each news story that you hear. Find out who the story is about, where it took place, what happened, why the event occurred, when the event occurred, and how the story happened and then ended. Use your notes to review the news broadcast for your class.**

_____

_____

_____

_____

Writing Prompt ● Writing Directions

Cooperative Group Activity

25. **Work with a group. Choose a process, such as going to a site on the Internet or making a recipe. Write detailed directions about how to complete the process. Exchange directions with another group and use each other's directions to complete the task chosen by the other group.**

_____

_____

_____

Speaking Prompt ● Examining a Job Application

Workplace Readiness Activity

26. **Work with a group. Get applications for several different jobs. Review each application, paying close attention to the different kinds of information requested on each. Work together to determine why the application for each type of job asks for a particular kind of information. Also determine why the applications are different, if they are. Give a brief presentation to the class concerning the information that is common to all the applications and the information that is specific to each kind of job. As a class, discuss why different kinds of information are required for different jobs.**

_____

_____

_____

Lesson 3

Classroom Discussion

Do you enjoy telling friends about the last movie that you saw? How do you describe the events of the story? How do you choose which details to include and which to leave out?

Classroom Activity

When you **paraphrase** a piece of writing, you retell it in your own words. Paraphrasing is an important skill when you are taking notes on what you read. As you note the central ideas and supporting details of a selection, always change the wording of the text. Later, when you use your notes to write a report or essay, you'll be sure not to plagiarize, or wrongfully copy, the words of someone else.

Read the following excerpt from Nathaniel Hawthorne's "The Ambitious Guest" and then answer the questions.

precipice– a steep overhanging rock

One September night a family had gathered round their hearth, and piled it high with the driftwood of mountain streams, the dry cones of the pine, and the splintered ruins of great trees that had come crashing down the precipice. Up the chimney roared the fire, and brightened the room with its broad blaze. The faces of the father and mother had a sober gladness; the children laughed; the eldest daughter was the image of happiness at seventeen; and the aged grandmother, who sat knitting in the warmest place, was the image of happiness grown old. They had found the "herb, heart's-ease," in the bleakest spot of all New England. This family was situated in the Notch of the White Hills, where the wind was sharp throughout the year, and pitilessly cold in the winter—giving their cottage all its fresh inclemency before it descended on the valley of the Saco. They dwelt in a cold spot and a dangerous one; for a mountain towered above their heads, so steep that the stones would often rumble down its sides and startle them at midnight.

inclemency– storminess or harshness

lamentation– great sadness

The daughter had just uttered some simple jest that filled them all with mirth, when the wind came through the Notch and seemed to pause before their cottage—rattling the door, with a sound of wailing and lamentation, before it passed into the valley. For a moment it saddened them, though there was nothing unusual in the tones. But the family were glad again when they perceived that the latch was lifted by some traveler, whose footsteps had been unheard amid the dreary blast which heralded his approach, and wailed as he was entering, and went moaning away from the door.

Though they dwelt in such a solitude, these people held daily converse with the world. . . When the footsteps were heard, therefore, between the outer door and the inner one, the whole family rose up, grandmother, children, and all, as if about to welcome someone who belonged to them, and whose fate was linked with theirs.

despondency– a state of hoplessness

The door was opened by a young man. His face at first wore the melancholy expression, almost despondency, of one who travels a wild and bleak road, at nightfall and alone, but soon brightened up when he saw the kindly warmth of his reception. He felt his heart spring forward to meet them all, from the old woman, who wiped a chair with her apron, to the little child that held out its arms to him. One glance and smile placed the stranger on a footing of innocent familiarity with the eldest daughter.

GO TO NEXT PAGE

"Ah, this fire is the right thing!" cried he; "especially when there is such a pleasant circle round it. I am quite benumbed; for the Notch is just like the pipe of a great bellows; it has blown a terrible blast in my face all the way from Bartlett."

"Then you are going toward Vermont?" said the master of the house, as he helped to take a light knapsack off the young man's shoulders.

"Yes; to Burlington, and far enough beyond," replied he. "I meant to have been at Ethan Crawford's tonight; but a pedestrian lingers along such a road as this. It is no matter; for, when I saw this good fire, and all your cheerful faces, I felt as if you had kindled it one purpose for me, and were waiting my arrival. So I shall sit down among you, and make myself at home."

The frank-hearted stranger had just drawn his chair to the fire when something like a heavy footstep was heard without, rushing down the steep side of the mountain, as with long and rapid strides, and taking such a leap in passing the cottage as to strike the opposite precipice. The family held their breath, because they knew the sound, and their guest held his by instinct.

"The old mountain has thrown a stone at us, for fear we should forget him," said the landlord, recovering himself. "He sometimes nods his head and threatens to come down; but we are old neighbors, and agree together pretty well on the whole. Besides, we have a sure place of refuge hard by if he should be coming in good earnest."

prophetic–
having to do with
foretelling the
future

Let us now suppose the stranger to have finished his supper of bear's meat; . . . He had traveled far and alone; his whole life, indeed, had been a solitary path; for, with the lofty caution of his nature, he had kept himself apart from those who might otherwise have been his companions. . . . But this evening a prophetic sympathy impelled the refined and educated youth to pour out his heart before the simple mountaineers, and constrained them to answer him with the same free confidence. And thus it should have been. Is not the kindred of a common fate a closer tie than that of birth?

The secret of the young man's character was a high and abstracted ambition. He could have borne to live an undistinguished life, but not to be forgotten in the grave. Yearning desire had been transformed to hope: and hope, long cherished, had become like certainty, that, obscurely as he journeyed now, a glory was to beam on all his pathway—though not, perhaps, while he was treading it. But when posterity should gaze back into the gloom of what was now the present, they would trace the brightness of his footsteps, brightening as meaner glories faded, and confess that a gifted one had passed from his cradle to his tomb with none to recognize him.

"As yet," cried the stranger—his cheek glowing and his eye flashing with enthusiasm—"as yet, I have done nothing. Were I to vanish from the earth tomorrow, none would know so much of me as you; that a nameless youth came up at nightfall from the valley of Saco, and opened his heart to you in the evening and passed through the Notch by sunrise, and was seen no more. Not a soul would ask, 'Who was he? Whither did the wanderer go?' But I cannot die till I have achieved my destiny. Then let death come! I shall have built my monument!"

Lesson 3

Step 1

Identify the central idea or theme of the first part of the story.

1. Why is danger and the possibility of death an important idea in this story?

_____

2. Why is ambition, or the desire to do something great and memorable, an important idea in this story?

_____

_____

3. What is the central idea or theme of this part of the story?

_____

_____

_____

Step 2

Identify a few of the main supporting details.

4. Who are the main characters in this story?

_____

_____

5. What dangers and discomforts do these characters face?

_____

_____

6. How do the family members react when they meet the stranger?

_____

7. What happens to remind everyone in the cottage about the steep mountain outside?

_____

8. What would happen to the people inside if a landslide fell on the cottage?

_____

9. What secret about himself does the young stranger tell the others?

_____

10. Has the young stranger accomplished anything great yet?

_____

Step 3

Use this information to write a paraphrase of this section of the story.

11. Which sentence would be best to begin a paraphrase of the beginning of the story?

a. A young traveler comes to a mountain cottage and begins telling everyone about the great things he will do someday.

b. One September night a family had gathered round their hearth, and piled it high with the driftwood of mountain streams, the dry cones of the pine, and the splintered ruins of great trees that had come crashing down the precipice.

c. A family lives in a cottage in a cold, dreary, and dangerous place at the foot of a steep mountain.

12. Why is answer b in question 11 not a good paraphrase of this story?

_____

13. Complete your paraphrase of the story here.

_____

_____

_____

_____

_____

_____

Open-Ended Question

14. Think about your answer to the following question. Write your answer on the lines. Be prepared to talk about your answer in a classroom discussion. Does every person have some ambition? Explain your answer.

_____

_____

_____

_____

_____

_____

Ideas to Remember

paraphrase—to retell in your own words the central idea and supporting details of material that you've read

Guided Practice Activity

Read this second excerpt from Nathaniel Hawthorne's "The Ambitious Guest." Answer the questions that follow.

"You laugh at me," said he, taking the eldest daughter's hand, and laughing himself. "You think my ambition is nonsensical as if I were to freeze myself to death on the top of Mount Washington, only that people might spy at me from the country round about. And, truly, that would be a noble pedestal for a man's statue!"

"It is better to sit here by this fire," answered the girl, blushing, "and be comfortable and contented, though nobody thinks about us."

"I suppose," said her father, after a fit of musing, "there is something natural in what the young man says; and if my mind had been turned that way, I might have felt just the same. It is strange, Wife, how his talk has set my head running on things that are pretty certain never to come to pass."

"Perhaps they may," observed the wife. "Is the man thinking what he will do when he is widower?"

"No, no!" cried he, repelling the idea with reproachful kindness. "When I think of your death, Esther, I think of mine too. But I was wishing we had a good farm in Bartlett, or Bethlehem, or Littleton, or some other township round the White Mountains; but not where they would tumble on our heads. I should want to stand well with my neighbors and be called Squire, and sent to General Court for a term or two; for a plain, honest man may do as much good there as a lawyer. And when I should be grown quite an old man, and you an old woman, so as not to be long apart, I might die happy enough in my bed, and leave you all crying around me. A slate gravestone would suit me as well as a marble one . . ."

"There, now!" exclaimed the stranger; "it is our nature to desire a monument, be it slate or marble, or a pillar of granite, or a glorious memory in the universal heart of man."

"We're in a strange way tonight," said the wife, with tears in her eyes. "They say it's a sign of something, when folks' minds go a-wandering so. Hark to the children!"

They listened accordingly. The younger children had been put to bed in another room, but with an open door between, so that they could be heard talking busily among themselves. One and all seemed to have caught the infection from the fireside circle, and were outvying each other in wild wishes, and childish projects of what they would do when they came to be men and women. At length a little boy, instead of addressing his brothers and sisters, called out to his mother.

outvying– outdoing

"I'll tell you what I wish, Mother," cried he. "I want you and Father and Grandma'am, and all of us, and the stranger, too, to start right away, and go and take a drink out of the basin of the Flume!"

Nobody could help laughing at the child's notion of leaving a warm bed, and dragging them from a cheerful fire, to visit the basin of the Flume—a brook which tumbles over the precipice, deep within the Notch. . . .

. . . The wind through the Notch took a deeper and drearier sound. It seemed, as the fanciful stranger said, like the choral strain of the spirits of the blast, who in old Indian times had their dwelling among these mountains, and made their heights and recesses a sacred region. There was a wail along the road, as if a funeral were passing. To chase away the gloom, the family threw pine branches on their fire, till the dry leaves crackled and the flame arose, discovering once again a scene of peace and humble happiness. The light hovered about them fondly, and caressed

GO TO NEXT PAGE

them all. There were the little faces of the children, peeping from their beds apart, and here the father's frame of strength, the mother's subdued and careful mien, the high-browed youth, the budding girl, and the good old grandam, still knitting in the warmest place. The aged woman looked up from her task, and with fingers ever busy, was the next to speak.

"Old folks have their notions," said she, "as well as young ones. You've been wishing and planning, and letting your heads run on one thing and another, till you've set my mind a-wandering too. Now what should an old woman wish for, when she can go but a step or two before she comes to her grave? Children, it will haunt me night and day till I tell you."

Then the old woman, with an air of mystery which drew the circle closer round the fire, informed them that she had provided her graveclothes some years before—a nice linen shroud, a cap with a muslin ruff, and everything of a finer sort that she had worn since her wedding day. But this evening an old superstition had strangely recurred to her. It used to be said, in her younger days, that if anything were amiss with a corpse, if only the ruff were not smooth, or the cap did not set right, the corpse in the coffin and beneath the clods would strive to put up its cold hands and arrange it. The bare thought made her nervous.

"Don't talk so, Grandmother!" said the girl, shuddering.

"Now," continued the old woman, with singular earnestness, yet smiling strangely at her own folly, "I want one of you to hold a looking glass over my face. Who knows but I may take a glimpse at myself, and see whether all's right?"

"Old and young, we dream of graves and monuments," murmured the stranger youth. . . .

Step 1

Identify the central idea or theme of the second part of the story.

15. What do the characters talk about in this section?

_____

_____

_____

_____

16. The young stranger says, "Old and young, we dream of graves and monuments." Use these words to help you write the central idea of the second part of the story.

_____

_____

_____

Language Arts

Lesson 3

Step 2

Identify the main supporting details.

17. Is the father happy with his life as it is?

_____

_____

18. Why does the young boy talk about going to drink water out of the mountain brook?

_____

_____

19. Why does the grandmother want someone to hold a looking glass, or mirror, over her face in the grave?

_____

_____

Step 3

Use this information to write a paraphrase of the second part of the story.

20. Which sentence best summarizes the ideas included in the second part of the story?

a. The family and the young stranger are worried about the rocks falling from the mountain and so they fall silent in the cottage.

b. After hearing the young stranger talk about ambition and death, the members of the family talk about their own wishes and plans.

c. The members of the family talk about how happy they are with their lives and how they can't imagine doing anything differently.

21. Write a short paraphrase of the second part of the story.

_____

_____

_____

_____

_____

_____

_____

Application Activity

Read the last part of Nathaniel Hawthorne's "The Ambitious Guest." Write a brief paragraph to paraphrase the last section. Then answer the questions that follow.

conception–
idea

For a moment, the old woman's ghastly conception so engrossed the minds of her hearers that a sound abroad in the night, rising like the roar of a blast, had grown broad, deep, and terrible, before the fated group were conscious of it. The house and all within it trembled; the foundations of the earth seemed to be shaken . . . Young and old exchanged one wild glance, and remained an instant, pale, affrighted, without utterance, or power to move. Then the same shriek burst simultaneously from all their lips.

"The slide! The slide!"

cataract–
downpour or flood

The simplest words must intimate, but not portray, the unutterable horror of the catastrophe. The victims rushed from their cottage, and sought refuge in what they deemed a safer spot—where, in contemplation of such an emergency, a sort of barrier had been reared. Alas! they had quitted their security, and fled right into the pathway of destruction. Down came the whole side of the mountain, in a cataract of ruin. Just before it reached the house, the stream broke into two branches—shivered not a window there, but overwhelmed the whole vicinity, blocked up the road, and annihilated everything in its dreadful course. Long ere the thunder of the great slide had ceased to roar among the mountains, the mortal agony had been endured, and the victims were at peace. Their bodies were never found.

The next morning, the light smoke was seen stealing from the cottage chimney up the mountainside. Within, the fire was yet smoldering on the hearth, and the chairs in a circle round it, as if the inhabitants had but gone forth to view the devastation of the slide, and would shortly return, to thank Heaven for their miraculous escape. All had left separate tokens, by which those who had known the family were made to shed a tear for each. Who has not heard their name? The story has been told far and wide, and will forever be a legend of these mountains. Poets have sung their fate.

There were circumstances which led some to suppose that a stranger had been received into the cottage on this awful night, and had shared the catastrophe of all its inmates. Others denied that there were sufficient grounds for such a conjecture. Woe for the high-souled youth, with his dream of earthly immortality! His name and person utterly unknown; his history, his way of life, his plans, a mystery never to be solved, his death and his existence equally a doubt! Whose was the agony of that death moment?

22. Write a paraphrase of the last part of the story here.

_____

_____

_____

_____

_____

_____

_____

Language Arts

Circle your answer to each question.

23. **Why were the family members and the young stranger slow to hear the sound of the landslide?**

    a. The sound was very faint.

    b. The people were laughing too hard.

    c. The wind was too loud.

    d. They were caught up in the grandmother's story.

24. **Why did the people in the cottage run outside when they heard the landslide?**

    a. to watch the landslide

    b. to seek refuge in a safer spot

    c. to run down the mountain

    d. to leap into the river

25. **Why was it a mistake for the people to run outside the cottage?**

    a. There was no landslide.

    b. The landslide missed the cottage.

    c. The cottage would have protected them from the landslide.

    d. The grandmother could not keep up with the others.

26. **Why was it ironic that the young man was talking about being remembered for some great deed?**

    a. He was killed just minutes later.

    b. He was already a famous artist.

    c. None of the family members believed his story.

    d. He could have lived happily with the family.

27. **The following is a sentence from the first part of the story: "When the footsteps were heard, therefore, between the outer door and the inner one, the whole family rose up, grandmother, children, and all, as if about to welcome someone who belonged to them, and whose fate was linked with theirs." What literary device is this an example of?**

    a. symbolism

    b. metaphor

    c. foreshadowing

    d. irony

28. **What do you think Nathaniel Hawthorne was saying about life and fate in this story?**

    _____

    _____

    _____

    _____

Open-Ended Question

29. **Use a separate piece of paper or write in your literary response journal. Refer to the information in this lesson.**

    ● What kind of deeds do you think the young stranger hoped to accomplish?

    ● How would you like to be remembered when you're gone?

Lesson 3

Extension Activities

Writing Prompt ● Paraphrasing a News Article

Individual
Activity

30. Choose a news article from your local newspaper. Read it carefully and make notes about the most important facts in the story. Then write a paraphrase of the article. Make sure you don't use the same wording as the reporter. Read over your paraphrase and correct any problems with grammar or wording. Check to see that you included the most important details. Is your paraphrase written as clearly as the original article?

_____

_____

_____

_____

Speaking Prompt ● Retelling a Story

Cooperative
Group
Activity

31. Work with a partner. Take turns retelling parts of "The Ambitious Guest" to each other. Imagine you're telling the story to someone who doesn't know what will happen. Try to include the most important details about character, setting, and plot. Have the person who is not retelling the story check the text to see that the details are correct. If possible, tape-record your retelling so that you can listen to yourself. Did you speak in complete sentences? Are your sentences arranged in a logical way? Are you speaking loudly enough to be heard easily by an audience?

_____

_____

_____

Viewing Prompt ● Demonstrate Skills Necessary for a Successful Job Interview

Workplace
Readiness
Activity

32. Work with a group. Discuss the communication skills needed for a successful job interview. For example, a job applicant should speak clearly while sitting up straight and looking the interviewer in the eyes. An applicant should answer each question fully and in concise language without rambling on or going off on a tangent. Have each member of the group write personal facts about himself or herself on a sheet of paper and read it over several times. Then role-play a job interview in which the interviewer asks for personal information such as job history, workplace goals, and outside interests. As each "applicant" answers the questions, he or she should paraphrase the facts that were written down. The interviewer might also ask follow-up questions so that the applicant can add information to their answers. After each role-played interview, discuss the applicant's performance and how it could be improved.

_____

_____

_____

 Language Arts

Recognition of Text Organization: Opening, Characters, Setting, Events, Closing

Classroom Discussion

What is your favorite movie? Who are the people in this movie? What happens to them during the story? What makes this your favorite movie?

Classroom Activity

Read and examine the following information. Answer the questions that follow.

Narratives, or pieces of fiction, are made up of elements that tell the story. Writers use these elements so that they affect readers, such as making readers feel suspense or humor or making a point about a person's life. Analyzing these story elements helps readers understand the story and how it is put together.

The first element of a story is the **opening**, which lets readers know how the story begins. Some stories grab readers with beginnings that include dramatic or exciting events. Others may begin slowly by describing a situation, a person in the story, or the place where the story occurs. The people in the story are the **characters**. The place and time where the story happens is the **setting**. The main things that happen during the story are the **events**. A series of events makes up the plot of the story. This series of events should lead the story to its **closing** or **ending**. An effective closing or ending should tie all the events together in a way that is believable.

Read the beginning of "The White Heron" by Sarah Orne Jewett. See if you can spot some of these story elements.

There was hardly a night the summer through when the old cow could be found waiting at the pasture bars; on the contrary, it was her greatest pleasure to hide herself away among the huckleberry bushes, and though she wore a loud bell she had made the discovery that if one stood perfectly still it would not ring. So Sylvia had to hunt for her until she found her, and call Co'! Co'! with never an answering Moo, until her childish patience was quite spent. If the creature had not given good milk and plenty of it, the case would have seemed very different to her owners. Besides, Sylvia had all the time there was, and very little use to make of it. Sometimes in pleasant weather it was a consolation to look upon the cow's pranks as an intelligent attempt to play hide and seek, and as the child had no playmates she lent herself to this amusement with a good deal of zest. Though this chase had been so long that the wary animal herself had given an unusual signal of her whereabouts, Sylvia had only laughed when she came upon Mistress Moolly at the swampside, and urged her affectionately homeward with a twig of birch leaves. The old cow was not inclined to wander farther, she even turned in the right direction for once as they left the pasture, and stepped along the road at a good pace. She was quite ready to be milked now, and seldom stopped to browse. Sylvia wondered what her grandmother would say because they were so late. It was a great while since she had left home at half-past five o'clock, but everybody knew the difficulty of making this errand a short one. Mrs. Tilley had chased the hornéd torment too many summer evenings herself to blame any one else for lingering, and was only thankful as she waited that she had Sylvia, nowadays, to give such valuable assistance. The good woman suspected that Sylvia loitered occasionally on her own account; there never was such a child for straying out-of-doors since the world was made! Everybody said that it was a good change for the little maid who had tried to grow for eight years in a crowded

GO TO NEXT PAGE

manufacturing town, but as for Sylvia herself, it seemed as if she never had been alive at all before she came to live at the farm. She thought often with wistful compassion of a wretched geranium that belonged to a town neighbor.

" 'Afraid of folks,' " old Mrs. Tilley said to herself, with a smile, after she had made the unlikely choice of Sylvia from her daughter's household of children, and was returning to the farm. " 'Afraid of folks,' they said! I guess she won't be troubled no great with 'em up to the old place!" When they reached the door of the lonely house and stopped to unlock it, and the cat came to purr loudly, and rub against them, . . . Sylvia whispered that this was a beautiful place to live in, and she never should wish to go home.

Step 1

Read and examine the opening of the story.

1. **What event opens the story?**

_____

_____

2. **How did Sylvia come to live in this place?**

_____

_____

Step 2

Make decisions about the characters and the setting.

3. **What two people are part of this story?**

_____

4. **What kind of person does Mrs. Tilley say that Sylvia is?**

_____

5. **Is Sylvia afraid of many things? How can you tell?**

_____

_____

6. **Where and when does this story take place?**

_____

Step 3

List the events that happen in the opening.

7. **What happens when Sylvia finds the cow?**

_____

_____

_____

Language Arts

8. How does this search affect her feelings about her home?

_____

_____

9. Why does Sylvia feel sorry for a geranium that belonged to a town neighbor?

_____

10. What does the last paragraph tell the reader about the early events of Sylvia's life?

_____

_____

Step 4

Think about the
way in which the
opening comes to
a close.

11. Why does Mrs. Tilley say that Sylvia will not be troubled by her fears of people after they reach the farm?

_____

12. How does the last sentence tell the reader about Sylvia's reactions to being taken from her home to a strange and lonely place?

_____

_____

Open-Ended
Question

13. Think about your answer to the following question. Write your answer on the lines. Be prepared to talk about your answer in a classroom discussion. How do you think your life would change if you were taken to live on Mrs. Tilley's farm?

_____

_____

_____

_____

_____

_____

_____

Ideas to Remember

opening–how a story begins

characters–the people who act out a story

setting–the place and time in which a story occurs

events–the main things that happen during a story. A series of events makes up the plot of the story

closing or ending–how the story comes to an end

Guided Practice Activity

On the way home with the cow, Sylvia meets a young man new to the area, who is looking for a place to stay. He walks her home, where Mrs. Tilley invites him to have supper and to spend the night.

It was a surprise to find so clean and comfortable a little dwelling in this New England wilderness. The young man had known the horrors of its most primitive housekeeping, and the dreary squalor of that level of society which does not rebel at the companionship of hens. This was the best thrift of an old-fashioned farmstead, though on such a small scale that it seemed like a hermitage. He listened eagerly to the old woman's quaint talk, he watched Sylvia's pale face and shining gray eyes with ever growing enthusiasm, and insisted that this was the best supper he had eaten for a month, and afterward the new-made friends sat down in the door-way together while the moon came up.

hermitage–
a place where a hermit lives

Soon it would be berry-time, and Sylvia was a great help at picking. The cow was a good milker, though a plaguy thing to keep track of, the hostess gossiped frankly, adding presently that she had buried four children, so Sylvia's mother, and a son (who might be dead) in California were all the children she had left. "Dan, my boy, was a great hand to go gunning," she explained sadly. "I never wanted for pa'tridges or gray squer'ls while he was home. He's been a great wand'rer, I expect, and he's no hand to write letters. There, I don't blame him, I'd ha' seen the world myself if it had been so I could."

"Sylvy takes after him," the grandmother continued affectionately, after a minute's pause. "There ain't a foot o' ground she don't know her way over, and the wild creaturs counts her one o' themselves. Squer'ls she'll tame to come an' feed right out o' her hands, and all sorts of birds. . . ."

"So Sylvy knows all about birds, does she!" he exclaimed, as he looked round at the little girl who sat, very demure, but increasingly sleepy, in the moonlight. "I am making a collection of birds myself. I have been at it every since I was a boy." (Mrs. Tilley smiled.) "There are two or three very rare ones I have been hunting for these five years. I mean to get them on my own ground if they can be found."

"Do you cage 'em up?" asked Mrs. Tilley doubtfully, in response to his enthusiastic announcement.

ornithologist–
an expert on birds

"Oh, no, they're stuffed and preserved, dozens and dozens of them," said the ornithologist, "and I have shot or snared every one myself. I caught a glimpse of a white heron a few miles from here on Saturday, and I have followed it in this direction. They have never been found in this district at all. The little white heron, it is," and he turned again to look at Sylvia with the hope of discovering that the rare bird was one of her acquaintances.

GO TO NEXT PAGE

 Language Arts

But Sylvia was watching a hop-toad in the narrow footpath.

"You should know the heron if you saw it," the stranger continued eagerly. "A queer tall white bird with soft feathers and long thin legs. And it would have a nest perhaps in the top of a high tree, made of sticks, something like a hawk's nest."

Sylvia's heart gave a wild beat; she knew that strange white bird, and had once stolen softly near where it stood in some bright green swamp grass, away over at the other side of the woods. There was an open place where the sunshine always seemed strangely yellow and hot, where tall, nodding rushes grew, and her grandmother warned her that she might sink in the soft black mud underneath and never be heard of more. Not far beyond were the salt marshes just this side the sea itself, which Sylvia wondered and dreamed much about, but never had seen, whose great voice could sometimes be heard above the noise of the woods on stormy nights.

"I can't think of anything I should like so much as to find that heron's nest," the handsome stranger was saying. "I would give ten dollars to anybody who could show it to me," he added desperately, "and I mean to spend my whole vacation hunting for it if need be. Perhaps it was only migrating, or had been chased out of its own region by some bird of prey."

divining–
understanding or
realizing

Mrs. Tilley gave amazed attention to all this, but Sylvia still watched the toad, not divining, as she might have done at some calmer time, that the creature wished to get to its hole under the door-step, and was much hindered by the unusual spectators at that hour of the evening. No amount of thought, that night, could decide how many wished-for treasures the ten dollars, so lightly spoken of, would buy.

The next day the young sportsman hovered about the woods, and Sylvia kept him company, having lost her first fear of the friendly lad, who proved to be most kind and sympathetic. He told her many things about the birds and what they knew and where they lived and what they did with themselves. And he gave her a jack-knife, which she thought as great a treasure as if she were a desert-islander. All day long he did not once make her troubled or afraid except when he brought down some unsuspecting singing creature from its bough. Sylvia would have liked him vastly better without his gun; she could not understand why he killed the very birds he seemed to like so much. But as the day waned, Sylvia still watched the young man with loving admiration. She had never seen anybody so charming and delightful; the woman's heart, asleep in the child, was vaguely thrilled by a dream of love. Some premonition of that great power stirred and swayed these young creatures who traversed the solemn woodlands with soft-footed silent care. They stopped to listen to a bird's song; they pressed forward again eagerly, parting the branches— speaking to each other rarely and in whispers, the young man going first and Sylvia following, fascinated, a few steps behind, with her gray eyes dark with excitement.

She grieved because the longed-for white heron was elusive, but she did not lead the guest, she only followed, and there was no such thing as speaking first. The sound of her own unquestioned voice would have terrified her—it was hard enough to answer yes or no when there was need of that. At last evening began to fall, and they drove the cow home together, and Sylvia smiled with pleasure when they came to the place where she heard the whistle and was afraid only the night before.

Lesson 4

Step 1

Read and examine the opening of the second part of the story.

14. Does the young man get along well with Sylvia and her grandmother? How can you tell?

_____

_____

_____

Step 2

Make decisions about the characters and the setting.

15. What character has been added at this point in the story?

_____

16. What kind of person does he seem to be?

_____

17. How are Sylvia and her grandmother different in dealing with the stranger?

_____

_____

18. Where and when does this part of the story take place?

_____

_____

Step 3

List the events in this part of the story.

19. Why has the young man come to this area?

_____

20. What does the reader learn about Mrs. Tilley's family from her conversation with the young man?

_____

_____

_____

21. Why does the young man offer a reward to Sylvia?

_____

22. Why is Sylvia so excited about the money?

_____

_____

 Language Arts

23. During the next day's search for the white heron, how does Sylvia come to feel about the young man?

_____

_____

_____

Step 4

Think about the way in which the second part of the story comes to a close.

24. Why does Sylvia grieve when they don't find the white heron?

_____

_____

25. Why do you think Sylvia becomes so attached to the young man?

_____

_____

Application
Activity

Now, read the ending of "The White Heron" by Sarah Orne Jewett. Answer the questions that follow.

Half a mile from home, at the farther edge of the woods, where the land was highest, a great pine-tree stood, the last of its generation. Whether it was left for a boundary mark, or for what reason, no one could say; the woodchoppers who had felled its mates were dead and gone long ago, and a whole forest of sturdy trees, pines and oaks and maples, had grown again. But the stately head of this old pine towered above them all and made a landmark for sea and shore miles and miles away. Sylvia knew it well. She had always believed that whoever climbed to the top of it could see the ocean; and the little girl had often laid her hand on the great rough trunk and looked up wistfully at those dark boughs that the wind always stirred, no matter how hot and still the air might be below. Now she thought of the tree with a new excitement, for why, if one climbed it at break of day could not one see all the world, and easily discover from whence the white heron flew, and mark the place, and find the hidden nest?

What a spirit of adventure, what wild ambition! What fancied triumph and delight and glory for the later morning when she could make known the secret! It was almost too real and too great for the childish heart to bear.

All night the door of the little house stood open and the whippoorwills came and sang upon the very step. The young sportsman and his old hostess were sound asleep, but Sylvia's great design kept her broad awake and watching. She forgot to think of sleep. The short summer night seemed as long as the winter darkness, and at last when the whippoorwills ceased, and she was afraid the morning would after all come too soon, she stole out of the house and followed the pasture path through the woods, hastening toward the open ground beyond, listening with a sense of comfort and companionship to the drowsy twitter of a half-awakened bird

GO TO NEXT PAGE

whose perch she had jarred in passing. Alas, if the great wave of human interest which flooded for the first time this dull little life should sweep away the satisfactions of an existence heart to heart with nature and the dumb life of the forest!

There was the huge tree asleep yet in the paling moonlight, and small and silly Sylvia began with utmost bravery to mount to the top of it, with tingling, eager blood coursing the channels of her whole frame, with her bare feet and fingers, that pinched and held like bird's claws to the monstrous ladder reaching up, up, almost to the sky itself. First she must mount the white oak tree that grew alongside, where she was almost lost among the dark branches and the green leaves heavy and wet with dew; a bird fluttered off its nest, and a red squirrel ran to and fro and scolded pettishly at the harmless housebreaker. Sylvia felt her way easily. She had often climbed there, and knew that higher still one of the oak's upper branches chafed against the pine trunk, just where its lower boughs were set close together. There, when she made the dangerous pass from one tree to the other, the great enterprise would really begin.

She crept out along the swaying oak limb at last, and took the daring step across into the old pine-tree. The way was harder than she thought; she must reach far and hold fast, the sharp dry twigs caught and held her and scratched her like angry talons, the pitch made her thin little fingers clumsy and stiff as she went round and round the tree's great stem, higher and higher upward. The sparrows and robins in the woods below were beginning to wake and twitter to the dawn, yet it seemed much lighter there aloft in the pine-tree, and the child knew she must hurry if her project were to be of any use.

The tree seemed to lengthen itself out as she went up, and to reach farther and farther upward. It was like a great main-mast to the voyaging earth; it must truly have been amazed that morning through all its ponderous frame as it felt this determined spark of human spirit wending its way from higher branch to branch. Who knows how steadily the least twigs held themselves to advantage this light, weak creature on her way! The old pine must have loved his new dependent. More than all the hawks, and bats, and moths, and even the sweet voiced thrushes, was the brave, beating heart of the solitary gray-eyed child. And the tree stood still and frowned away the winds that June morning while the dawn grew bright in the east.

Sylvia's face was like a pale star, if one had seen it from the ground, when the last thorny bough was past, and she stood trembling and tired but wholly triumphant, high in the treetop. Yes, there was the sea with the dawning sun making a golden dazzle over it, and toward that glorious east flew two hawks with slow-moving pinions. How low they looked in the air from that height when one had only seen them before far up, and dark against the blue sky. Their gray feathers were as soft as moths; they seemed only a little way from the tree, and Sylvia felt as if she too could go flying away among the clouds. Westward, the woodlands and farms reached miles and miles into the distance; here and there were church steeples, and white villages, truly it was a vast and awesome world!

The birds sang louder and louder. At last the sun came up bewilderingly bright. Sylvia could see the white sails of ships out at sea, and the clouds that were purple and rose-colored and yellow at first began to fade away. Where was the white heron's nest in the sea of green branches, and was this wonderful sight and pageant of the world the only reward for having climbed to such a giddy height? Now look down again, Sylvia, where the green marsh is set among the shining birches and dark hemlocks; there where you saw the white heron once you will see him again; look, look! a white spot of him like a single floating feather comes up from the dead hemlock and grows larger, and rises, and comes close at last, and goes by the landmark pine with steady sweep of wing and outstretched slender neck and crested head. And wait! wait! do not move a foot or a finger, little girl, do not send an arrow of light and consciousness from your two eager eyes, for the heron has perched on a pine bough not far beyond yours, and cries back to his mate on the nest and plumes his feathers for the new day!

The child gives a long sigh a minute later when a company of shouting cat-birds comes also to the tree, and vexed by their fluttering and lawlessness the solemn heron goes away. She knows his secret now, the wild, light, slender bird that floats and wavers and goes back like an arrow presently to his home in the green world beneath. Then Sylvia, well satisfied, makes her perilous way down again, not daring to look far below the branch she stands on, ready to cry sometimes because her fingers ache and her lamed feet slip. Wondering over and over again what the stranger would say to her, and what he would think when she told him how to find his way straight to the heron's nest.

"Sylvy, Sylvy!" called the busy old grandmother again and again, but nobody answered, and the small husk bed was empty and Sylvia had disappeared.

The guest waked from a dream, and remembering his day's pleasure hurried to dress himself that might it sooner begin. He was sure from the way the shy little girl looked once or twice yesterday that she had at least seen the white heron, and now she must really be made to tell. Here she comes now, paler than ever, and her worn old frock is torn and tattered, and smeared with pine pitch. The grandmother and the sportsman stand in the door together and question her, and the splendid moment has come to speak of the dead hemlock-tree by the green marsh.

But Sylvia does not speak after all, though the old grandmother fretfully rebukes her, and the young man's kind, appealing eyes are looking straight in her own. He can make them rich with money; he has promised it, and they are poor now. He is so well worth making happy, and he waits to hear the story she can tell.

No, she must keep silence! What is it that suddenly forbids her and makes her dumb? Has she been nine years growing and now, when the great world for the first time puts out a hand to her, must she thrust it aside for a bird's sake? The murmur of the pine's green branches is in her ears, she remembers how the white heron came flying through the golden air and how they watched the sea and the morning together, and Sylvia cannot speak; she cannot tell the heron's secret and give its life away.

Dear loyalty, that suffered a sharp pang as the guest went away disappointed later in the day, that could have served and followed him and loved him as a dog loves! Many a night Sylvia heard the echo of his whistle haunting the pasture path as she came home with the loitering cow. She forgot even her sorrow at the sharp report of his gun and the sight of thrushes and sparrows dropping silent to the ground, their songs hushed and their pretty feathers stained and wet with blood. Were the birds better friends than their hunter might have been,—who can tell? Whatever treasures were lost to her, woodlands and summer-time, remember! Bring your gifts and graces and tell your secrets to this lonely country child!

Circle your answer to each question.

26. What do you learn about the setting in the first paragraph of this part of the story?
a. This area is surrounded by wilderness that has rarely been explored.
b. The area has changed very little over the centuries.
c. Most people in the area make their livings by cutting trees for the lumber industry.
d. It is an area of woods and marshes near the ocean.

27. Which character is not featured in this part of the story?
a. Mrs. Tilley   c. Sylvia
b. Mr. Tilley   d. the young man

28. Which of the following events happens first?
a. Sylvia lays awake all night thinking of ways to find the white heron's nest.
b. Sylvia climbs the ancient pine tree to get a look at the woods.
c. Sylvia experiences the wonder of the sunrise over the ocean.
d. Sylvia sees the white heron rise from its nest in the dead hemlock tree.

29. What proves Sylvia's bravery and determination?
a. speaking so strongly to the young man
b. climbing the ancient pine tree
c. killing the cat-birds that are raiding the white heron's nest
d. saving the young man from falling out of the tree

30. Which of the following does NOT describe an emotion felt by Sylvia while viewing the world from the top of the tree?
a. fear   c. wonder
b. awe   d. love

31. Why does Sylvia let the young man leave without telling how to find the white heron?
a. She has learned to hate guns.
b. She realizes he has no money to pay the reward.
c. She does not want the white heron to be killed.
d. She knows that her grandmother will take away the reward if she earns it.

32. What played the greatest part in Sylvia's decision?
a. her deep concern for the welfare of her family
b. her desire for love and companionship
c. her love for the woods and its creatures
d. her unwillingness to disappoint another human being

Open-Ended
Question

33. Use a separate piece of paper or write in your literary response journal. Refer to the information in this lesson.

● Why does Sarah Orne Jewett say that the woodlands and summer should bring their gifts, graces, and secrets to Sylvia?

● Would you like to have a person like Sylvia as a friend? Why or why not?

Extension Activities

Reading Prompt ● Organization of a Short Story

Individual Activity

34. Check out a book of short stories from the library or reexamine books that you have already read. How does the story open? What important facts are described in the opening? Who are the main characters? What do the events of the story tell you about the characters and their feelings? What is the setting of the story? How does it affect the characters and events? What are the main events of the story in order? How did the ending or closing tie the events together? Write a short report about the short story or book. Tell whether you would recommend the book to others and why.

_____

_____

_____

_____

Viewing Prompt ● Analyzing Story Elements in Movies

Cooperative Group Activity

35. Work with a small group. Talk about some of your favorite movies. Which of the story elements that you studied in this lesson were included in these movies? How did the elements affect the stories and the action that takes place? Which elements were conveyed effectively by the actions and events depicted in these movies? Why are actions and events important in conveying the point of a movie? Why do you think most movies involve many of the same elements as stories?

_____

_____

_____

_____

Writing Prompt ● Using Critical-Thinking Skills

Workplace Readiness Activity

36. Work with a group. Go online and search the Internet or conduct research in the school or community library. What kinds of jobs involve writing about events and actions? Examine such jobs as those held by psychiatrists, insurance examiners, doctors, police officers, fire fighters, news reporters, and others. Which of these workers would benefit from a sound knowledge of story elements? How would each kind of worker use some or all of these elements in doing his or her job? Why would a writing style that is simple and easy to understand be valuable in these jobs? Write a group report that presents your findings.

_____

_____

_____

_____

Classroom
Discussion

Do you read fiction or nonfiction? What kinds of fiction do you enjoy the most? Why do some writers and speakers prepare works of nonfiction?

Classroom
Activity

Read the following information and answer the questions in the boxes.

Some writers prepare **nonfiction** materials that **inform** their readers, or present facts and details about real people, events, and ideas. This kind of writing involves thorough research so that the material is accurate. Research is also required for pieces of fiction. A writer or speaker may place their ideas or events during a particular time in history. It is important that all the details are historically accurate so that the audience clearly understands what the writer or speaker is trying to convey. Sometimes material is prepared to **entertain** an audience, or make them laugh, feel sad, or experience suspense. Writing or speaking intended to **persuade** tries to convince an audience to accept an idea or suggestion. Other kinds of writing can **instruct**, or explain how something is done, such as in a set of directions.

Which ideas help you identify the purpose of the author who wrote the following report?

After hatching and raising their young during the warm summer months, birds migrate to escape the harsh conditions of winter. Millions of birds around the world make these trips that cross not only continents, but sometimes oceans as well. The blackpoll warbler builds its nest and raises its young in North America during the spring and summer months. By fall, the young are grown and have left to begin lives of their own. At that time, blackpoll warblers begin one of the most amazing journeys in nature. These birds take to the air and begin to fly south. For 90 hours they continue flying south out of North America and into Central and South America. At the end of about three-and-one-half days, the birds reach their winter home in South America, 2,500 miles away from where their trip began. None of the birds stops, eats, drinks, or takes a rest during the entire trip. The blackpoll warbler is the only one of the smaller birds to make nonstop migrations. Usually only the largest birds can make such trips.

The Arctic tern holds the record for distance among the migration patterns of birds. It builds its nest and raises its young in the Arctic during the short period of warm weather and daylight during spring and summer. Then, the Arctic tern begins a trip to the other end of the world, Antarctica. This continent also has spring and summer seasons that last for only a few months. Before long, the Arctic tern makes the journey back to the Arctic. Each leg of this trip covers about 11,000 miles. These birds have an amazing sense of direction, since they usually return to the exact spot in the Arctic each year to build their nests.

                    Language Arts

Step 1

Identity the topic of this material.

1. **What is the topic of these two paragraphs?**

_____

Step 2

Locate the central idea and supporting details of this material.

2. **What sentence states the central idea of this material?**

_____

3. **Why do birds migrate?**

_____

4. **What makes the migration of the blackpoll warbler so amazing?**

_____

5. **How have the migratory habits of the Arctic tern helped it set a record?**

_____

_____

_____

Step 3

Analyze the topic, central idea, and facts, and identify the writer's or speaker's purpose.

6. **What does this paragraph tell you about birds? Circle your answer.**
   a. Birds migrate along routes that carry them extremely long distances.
   b. All the largest birds make trips of about 11,000 miles each year when they migrate.
   c. To escape the harsh conditions of the winter season, different birds carry out different migratory habits.

7. **What is the purpose of this report? Circle the letter of your answer.**
   a. persuade   c. entertain
   b. inform   d. instruct

Open-Ended Question

8. Think about your answer to the following question. Write your answer on the lines. Be prepared to talk about your answer in a classroom discussion. What are different reasons that humans make long trips from one region to another or from one continent to another?

_____

_____

_____

_____

Ideas to Remember

purpose–the reason for doing something

inform–to present facts and details about real people, events, and ideas

entertain–to present material so that an audience laughs, feels sad, or experiences suspense

persuade–to try to convince an audience to accept an idea or suggestion

instruct–to explain to an audience how something is done

Guided Practice Activity

Read the paragraph below. Then follow the steps and answer the questions in the boxes.

Birds want to keep their whereabouts secret so that their nest, eggs, and young are safe from predators and other dangers. Birds can be difficult to study because their nests are often very difficult to find. How can you locate nests in your neighborhood each spring so that you can study local birds and their nesting habits? You will need some wire mesh, pliers or snips, strands of wire that are easy to bend, and cotton. Use pliers or snips to cut two circles out of the wire mesh. Make sure each circle is three inches across. Now cut out a square of mesh and wrap it around the circles to form a cylinder that is about six inches long. Use the strands of wire to attach the circles to the square mesh to form the cylinder. Before you close up the last circle to form the cylinder, fill the cylinder with cotton. Once the cylinder is complete, hang it from the limb of a tree or bush. Birds will be attracted to the cotton fibers, which they will gather as building materials for their nests. Look for spots of white color in trees and bushes. These should be patches of cotton used to make birds' nests. Once you have located the nests, keep an eye on the birds and their habits. Remember, if you touch the nest or eggs, the parents will identify the scent of humans and abandon the nest, and the eggs will never hatch. Young birds that have been touched with human hands will also be abandoned by their parents. Take special care that you do not bring harm to these special animals.

Step 1

Identity the topic of this material.

9. What is the topic of these two paragraphs?

Step 2

Locate the central idea and supporting details of this material.

10. What sentence states the central idea of this material?

11. Why do birds try to hide their nests?

12. How will a cylinder of cotton help in locating and studying birds?

_____

_____

13. What materials are needed to make this kind of cylinder?

_____

14. Why does the author urge people not to touch nests, eggs, or young birds?

_____

_____

Step 3

Analyze the topic, central idea, and facts, and identify the writer's or speaker's purpose.

15. What does this paragraph tell you about birds? Circle your answer.
   a. Birds and their nests are difficult to locate and study, and should never be touched or bothered.
   b. Birds are among nature's most difficult creatures to study.
   c. Birds and their nesting habits are among the most fascinating studies that can be conducted in nature.

16. What is the purpose of the section that describes the cotton-filled wire cylinder? Circle your answer.

   a. persuade   c. entertain
   b. inform   d. instruct

17. What is the purpose of the section that describes the harm that can be caused by touching birds, nests, eggs, and young birds? Circle your answer.

   a. persuade   c. entertain
   b. inform   d. instruct

Application Activity

Read the story below. Answer the questions that follow.

There are as many kinds of nests as there are kinds of birds. Birds' nests are so distinctive that the ways in which they are constructed tells ornithologists, or scientists who study birds, what kind of bird was the builder. Most are built in the usual dish-shaped form that is usually associated with bird nests. However, the size, materials and exact shape vary from one kind of bird to another. Robins build such nests out of grass. The grass is coated with mud not only to hold the grass together but to attach the nest to the branch that is its foundation. The grass and mud act as insulation, helping the mother keep her eggs warm. Once the eggs have hatched, the insulating characteristics

GO TO NEXT PAGE

of the nest protect the young birds while the mother collects food for her family. Baltimore orioles build nests that are dish-shaped like robins' nests. However, orioles do not place their nests on branches or other solid surfaces as foundations. Orioles' nests are built with special straps that allow the nest to hang from a branch. The saucer becomes more like a pouch that keeps the eggs and young hidden from predators and the rest of the world. Some birds, like swallows and phoebes, use mud as a glue for their nests. The mud holds the nest together, but it also fastens them to the sides of trees or barns, or to the tops of walls and other structures. These sturdy nests provide strong protection from enemies.

Most animals probably began building nests by scooping out holes in the ground. The holes kept the eggs in one place, and the earth helped to keep them warm. Such nests were not very secure from attacks by snakes, different forms of cats, large meat-eating birds, and other predators. To make the nests difficult to reach and destroy, most birds began building their homes high above the ground in places that were hard for nonflying animals to reach. One exception is the quail, which builds a nest of grasses and twigs but places it on the ground. Such nests are constructed in grassy or woody areas of materials that grow locally. The natural substances cause the nests to blend in with their surroundings, camouflaging them from the dangers that exist in nature. Hummingbirds also build nests that are carefully camouflaged. Since hummingbirds are among the smallest of birds, they build some of the smallest nests. These nests are cunningly built to look like the knots seen on tree trunks or branches. Each hummingbird egg weighs about 1/50 of an ounce, so a clutch, or batch of eggs laid at one time, will fill a nest that would be very hard to spot indeed.

A few birds do not build nests at all, but take over nests built by other birds. For example, starlings will even chase birds from their nests and then take over the structures for their own use. Penguins in Antarctica do not build nests since there are few materials available or high places in which to locate these homes. Instead, penguins hold their eggs on the tops of their feet. The male holds the egg in place by hunkering its warm tummy over the eggs. The warmth from the father's body incubates the eggs until they hatch and then protects the young from the cold. During all this time, the father will not leave the egg. The fathers does not eat until the female penguin returns from her fishing trip in the ocean. The well-fed female uses the food stored in her stomach to raise the young to the point where they can care for themselves. When the female returns, the male goes to sea so he can catch fish and feed himself.

Through the years, advances in technology have caused some surprising curiosities to develop in birds' nests. California's utility poles became riddled with holes dug out by woodpeckers, who build nests inside wooden cavities. Now, the energy companies are using steel for their new poles. However, the old wooden poles are not being completely removed. Many are being left in place to provide locations for future woodpecker homes. Some birds use manufactured products in building their nests. Nests made up almost entirely of facial tissue have been built by warbling vireos. Bread wrappers, newspapers, string, and pieces of plastic have been found woven into the structure of nests. One Minnesota brown thrasher found a United States five-dollar bill and wove it into its nest. In California, a nest was built by canyon wrens entirely from manufactured goods they had located as litter. The nest weighed almost three pounds because it was made of metal products like paper clips, pins, rubber bands, and thumbtacks. To explore the mysteries of the universe, you should begin with a study of the birds that live in your own backyard.

Language Arts

Circle the letter of your answer for each question.

18. What is the topic of this report or speech?
   a. the ways in which birds raise their young
   b. the nesting habits of birds
   c. the history of nests and why they are built
   d. the wonders of nature's flying organisms

19. What is the central idea of this material?
   a. Birds are the only animals in nature that build their own homes.
   b. Each kind of nest and its materials are unique to each kind of bird.
   c. Few of the earth's living organisms have been as thoroughly studied as birds.
   d. An area and its surroundings help determine the kinds of nests that birds will build.

20. Which of the following is NOT a purpose for a nest?
   a. storage for food
   b. warmth for eggs and young
   c. protection from predators
   d. safety from bad weather

21. Why must the materials for an oriole's nest be especially strong?
   a. because the nest is built on the ground
   b. because the eggs of an oriole are so heavy
   c. because the oriole lays so many eggs at one time
   d. because it must hang from the branches of a tree without falling

22. How does camouflage help protect a nest?
   a. by making the nest tough and sturdy to protect it from predators
   b. by making the nest difficult for predators to reach
   c. by making the nest difficult for predators to see
   d. by providing the nest with openings that are easy to close

23. Why do male penguins refuse to eat while tending their eggs?
   a. so that the eggs are not easy prey for predators
   b. so that the eggs do not become too cold
   c. so that the eggs are not left out on the open ground
   d. all of the above

24. Where do birds get things like paper clips and rubber bands to make their nests?
   a. They dig in trash cans.   c. They take them from inside the houses.
   b. They find them on the ground as litter   d. They find them at the dump.

Write your answers on the lines following each question.

25. What kind of person prepared this material? How can you tell?

_____

_____

26. What is the author's purpose in writing this material?

_____

_____

27. What is the purpose of the author's last line?

_____

_____

_____

Open-Ended Question

28. Use a separate piece of paper or write in your literary response journal. Refer to the information in the story.

- Why do you think that different kinds of birds have developed different kinds of habits, nests, and parenting techniques?

- What kinds of factors do you think might cause birds to change their habits?

Extension Activities

Reading Prompt ● Analyzing Periodicals

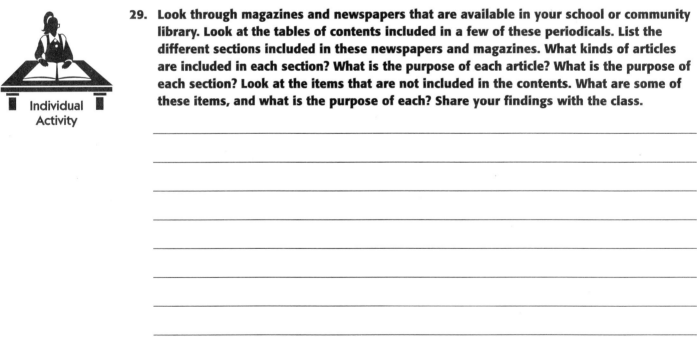

29. Look through magazines and newspapers that are available in your school or community library. Look at the tables of contents included in a few of these periodicals. List the different sections included in these newspapers and magazines. What kinds of articles are included in each section? What is the purpose of each article? What is the purpose of each section? Look at the items that are not included in the contents. What are some of these items, and what is the purpose of each? Share your findings with the class.

Individual Activity

 Language Arts

Listening Prompt ● Identifying the Speaker's Purpose

Cooperative
Group
Activity

30. Work with a group. Find an all-news channel on a television kept in your classroom, school library, or other school location. Talk about each person who helps present the news. What kinds of reports do they make? What are the topics and central ideas or themes of each report? What is the purpose of each report? Do any of the presenters express opinions about these reports? What are these opinions? Why do you think the producers included these people and their opinions as part of the program?

_____

_____

_____

_____

_____

_____

_____

_____

Writing Prompt ● Using Critical-Thinking Skills

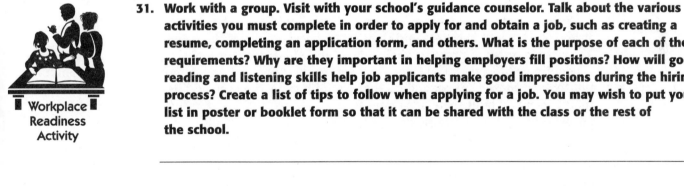

Workplace
Readiness
Activity

31. Work with a group. Visit with your school's guidance counselor. Talk about the various activities you must complete in order to apply for and obtain a job, such as creating a resume, completing an application form, and others. What is the purpose of each of these requirements? Why are they important in helping employers fill positions? How will good reading and listening skills help job applicants make good impressions during the hiring process? Create a list of tips to follow when applying for a job. You may wish to put your list in poster or booklet form so that it can be shared with the class or the rest of the school.

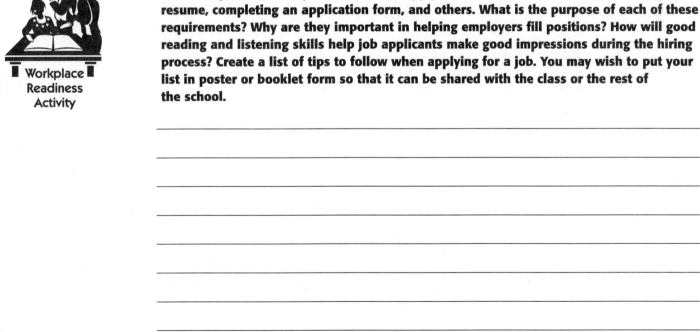

_____

_____

_____

_____

_____

_____

_____

_____

Classroom Discussion

A flying saucer has landed in your backyard, and its crew is planning a visit that will last a full day. What will you tell the television crews that will arrive to cover the story? How will you make sure that you leave nothing out when you talk to the reporters about your adventure?

Classroom Activity

Read and examine the information below. Answer the questions that follow.

To make sure that all the necessary information is included in a piece of writing or a speech, the author must answer these questions—*Who, What, When, Where, Why, and How*, known as *the Five W's and the H*. While reading a report or listening to a presentation, you need to answer these questions, too. This will help you understand what the writer or speaker is trying to convey. Read the following article and look for the most important facts.

Among the Native Americans who first lived in what is now the Southeastern United States were the Cherokees. These people hunted and farmed in the Appalachian area that became Tennessee, Georgia, and Alabama. From the early 1600s to the middle 1700s, Europeans came to the area to settle. To protect their homes and land, the Cherokees fought back. When the Revolutionary War began in 1775, the Cherokees decided to join in the war. They became allies of the British, who were fighting to keep their 13 colonies from becoming independent of Britain. In exchange for the Cherokees' support in winning the war, the British promised to preserve the Cherokees' claim to the ancient lands.

Britain lost the Revolutionary War, however, and British support for the Cherokees disappeared. The Cherokees and their lands became part of the new United States of America. In order to preserve their homes and identity as a people, many Cherokees began to adopt new lifestyles. The Cherokees set up their own form of democratic government and took on those European ideas that would benefit the area and its people. By the early 1800s, they had built thriving communities, rich plantations, and fine homes throughout the area. Some became so rich that they owned slaves and built beautiful mansions similar to those owned by wealthy Americans. Other groups who followed this plan were the Choctaws, Chickasaws, Creeks, and Seminoles. Along with these groups, the Cherokees became known as the Five Civilized Tribes.

Step 1

Identify the topic of this material.

> **1. What groups of people are described in these two paragraphs?**
>
> _____
>
> **2. Which one group is the main focus of this material?**
>
> _____

Language Arts

Step 2

Identify where and when the action happened.

3. **Where did the Cherokees live?**

_____

4. **When did the events in the article take place?**

_____

Step 3

Identify how and why the events in these paragraphs happened.

5. **Why did the Cherokees decide to support the British in the Revolutionary War?**

_____

6. **How did the Cherokees support the British?**

_____

7. **How did the Cherokees change their lives?**

_____

_____

8. **Why did the Cherokees and the other Civilized Tribes make these kinds of changes?**

_____

Open-Ended Question

9. Think about your answer to the following question. Write your answer on the lines. Be prepared to talk about your answer in a classroom discussion. How would you describe the actions and achievements of the Cherokee people?

_____

_____

_____

_____

_____

_____

_____

_____

Ideas to Remember

Five W's and the H—questions that help a reader or listener gather the facts

Guided Practice Activity

Read the next part of the article. Think about the Five *W's and the H* as you read. Answer the questions that follow.

Europeans continued to arrive in the United States after the Revolutionary War. Veterans of the war had been promised free land by the government. Americans began looking west of the original 13 colonies for areas into which they could expand. These lands had already been settled by the Five Civilized Tribes. When gold was discovered on Cherokee land in 1828, thousands of Americans flocked to the area. Disputes over land become so severe that the United States government began negotiations with the Five Civilized Tribes. In 1835, a few groups within the Five Civilized Tribes signed a treaty in which they agreed that all the Five Civilized Tribes would move west into areas that are now Arkansas, Kansas, and Oklahoma. Some packed up their belongings and made the long trip to their new homes.

However, most of the Five Civilized Tribes refused to honor the treaty. Their leaders took the fight against the treaty to Washington, D.C. A lawsuit was filed, and it eventually reached the Supreme Court. According to the Supreme Court, the ideas in the treaty went against the U.S. Constitution. The Court ruled that the treaty was not valid. However, President Andrew Jackson and most of the government disagreed with this decision. In the winter of 1838, President Jackson sent the U.S. Army to force the Five Civilized Tribes to leave their lands and to move west. The Native Americans were rounded up and given no time to pack their belongings. The people, who had little food or gear, were marched westward along what became known as The Trail of Tears. By the time they reached their new lands in 1839, thousands of Cherokees, Choctaws, Chickasaws, Creeks, and Seminoles had died.

Step 1

Identify the topic of this material.

10. What group of people is the main focus of these two paragraphs?

_____

Step 2

Identify where and when the action happened.

11. Where was gold found?

_____

12. When was the gold found?

_____

13. How long did the events in this part of the article last?

_____

Language Arts

Lesson 6

Step 3

Identify how and why the events in these paragraphs happened.

14. How did the discovery of gold affect Americans and the people of the Five Civilized Tribes?

_____

_____

15. How did different groups in the Five Civilized Tribes react to the treaty signed in 1835?

_____

16. How did different groups in the United States government react to the treaty signed in 1835?

_____

_____

17. Why did President Jackson send the U.S. Army into the lands of the Five Civilized Tribes?

_____

18. Why did so many Native Americans die during the march westward?

_____

19. Why was the route of this trip called The Trail of Tears?

_____

_____

Application Activity

Read the story below. Answer the questions that follow.

Near the town of Rocky Mountain, Oklahoma, is a place called Mankiller Flats. This place was the home of the Mankiller family, descendants of the Cherokees who traveled along The Trail of Tears. On November 18, 1945, a little girl who would bring about great changes for the Cherokees was born to this family. She was given the name Wilma Pearl Mankiller. Her grandfather had received the 160 acres of Mankiller Flats in 1907, when Indian Territory and Oklahoma Territory were combined to form the state of Oklahoma. The Native Americans who had lived in these territories had once been sovereign nations and had governed themselves. When statehood came, all the lands of the reservations were divided among the members. They became citizens of the new state.

In the 1950s, the United States government began a program to assimilate Native Americans into modern American life. Tribes were broken up, and families were moved to different locations. Wilma Mankiller's family was moved from Oklahoma to San Francisco, California in 1956. They had been a poor family living in a rural area. They became a poor family living in an urban area. Mr. Mankiller did find work, but it was usually in low-paying jobs. One benefit of the government's program was the creation of a college fund for Native Americans. Wilma Mankiller earned a degree from San Francisco State University in social science, a degree which would enable her to help people and improve their lives.

GO TO NEXT PAGE

Application Activity

During the 1970s, many Native American groups began pushing for civil rights and for the federal government to honor the terms of the treaties it had signed over two centuries. One treaty stated that Native Americans could take over ownership of government lands that had been abandoned. Alcatraz Prison was a federal penitentiary on an island in San Francisco Bay. It had been shut down for many years; Native Americans petitioned for ownership of the island and its buildings. When the federal government refused, many Native Americans moved to the island in 1970 and refused to leave. In time, federal marshals forced the Native Americans to leave the island, but the country was now aware of the new efforts by Native Americans to take control of their lives. The experience galvanized the Mankiller family, some of whom participated in the occupation of Alcatraz Island. Wilma Mankiller joined the push for civil rights and became a member of the American Indian Movement (AIM). Politics would become an important part of her life.

Ms. Mankiller's life changed even more when she moved back to Oklahoma with her daughters in 1976. She obtained a job with the government of the Cherokee nation. In 1970, the U.S. government had given up control of the various tribes, who were allowed to elect their own chiefs and set up their own governments. Wilma Mankiller worked to obtain government grants of money that could be used to help the Cherokee Nation. Even a near-fatal car wreck in 1979 could not stop this incredible woman from working to help her people. The wreck and the consequent seventeen operations barely kept her from her office. In 1981, she took on the job of rebuilding the Cherokee community of Bell, Oklahoma. With private money and Cherokee volunteers, Ms. Mankiller led the Cherokees in repairing and constructing buildings, homes, and businesses. The project was such a huge success that Principal Chief Ross Swimmer invited Wilma Mankiller to run as his Deputy Chief. Despite great opposition to a woman holding this job, the two won their offices in 1983. Wilma Mankiller would hold her position for only two years.

Ross Swimmer resigned his position as Principal Chief in 1986. President Ronald Reagan selected Swimmer to become the new head of the Bureau of Indian Affairs in Washington, D.C. According to the Cherokee Constitution, Wilma Mankiller became the first woman Principal Chief of the Cherokees in 1986. She subsequently was elected to two terms in office, which she held in all for 10 years. Her work in making successes of Cherokee businesses allowed the Cherokee Nation to build medical clinics and offer jobs to members of the tribe. During her years as leader, the Cherokee Nation tripled in numbers and doubled its budget. It became successful not only in business and government, but also in preserving the basic ideals that make up the native culture of the Cherokees. This work and other achievements helped Wilma Mankiller become one of the most admired people not only among her people but throughout the United States.

As Principal Chief, Wilma Mankiller faced adversity as well as success. In 1990, a hereditary condition made it necessary for Chief Mankiller to undergo a kidney transplant. Her work continued despite her medical problems, and when she retired in 1996, she was recognized and admired all over the country. Since that time she has been busy with a career that continues to help Native Americans. In 1998, Wilma Mankiller received the country's highest civilian honor, the Medal of Freedom, from President Bill Clinton, who called her "a revered leader who built a brighter and healthier future for her nation. When she stepped down as chief, the Cherokee Nation wept." However, Ms. Mankiller says that she is just an ordinary person who has been fortunate to have had many wonderful experiences.

GO TO NEXT PAGE

Circle your answers to these questions.

20. Who is the topic of this story?

   a. Ross Swimmer

   b. Wilma Mankiller

   c. Bill Clinton

   d. Ronald Reagan

21. What is the central idea of this story?

   a. Wilma Mankiller achieved success as the first woman to hold the post of Principal Chief of the Cherokee Nation.

   b. An early interest in politics helped Wilma Mankiller succeed as a member of the Cherokee Nation.

   c. Wilma Mankiller has overcome many problems in her life.

   d. In spite of great adversity like poverty and illness, Wilma Mankiller's strength of character has made her a great leader.

22. When did Wilma Mankiller first become involved in political work to help change the lives of Native Americans?

   a. 1945

   b. 1956

   c. 1970

   d. 1981

23. Where did Wilma Mankiller decide her life should be centered after 1976?

   a. with the Cherokee Nation of Oklahoma

   b. with the occupation of Alcatraz Island

   c. with the government of the Cherokee Nation

   d. with the people of northeastern Oklahoma

24. Why did Ross Swimmer think that Ms. Mankiller would be a good candidate for Deputy Chief?

   a. because of her success in obtaining millions of dollars in federal grants

   b. because of her success in dealing with Native Americans and their medical problems

   c. because of her ability to lead the people in revitalizing Bell, Oklahoma

   d. because of her ability to continue working in spite of illness and hardship

25. How did Wilma Mankiller affect the Cherokee Nation as its Principal Chief?

   a. by increasing the success of Cherokee businesses

   b. by building medical clinics for the people

   c. by helping preserve the culture of the Cherokees

   d. all of the above

Write answers for each of the following questions.

26. How do you think people's ideas about women as leaders changed after Wilma Mankiller's years as Principal Chief?

_____

_____

27. What are the characteristics of Wilma Mankiller's personality and character that have made her such a successful person?

_____

_____

Open-Ended Question

28. Use a separate piece of paper or write in your literary response journal. Refer to the information in the story.

- How do you think the events of Wilma Mankiller's early life affected her success as an adult?

- Do you agree with the idea that facing and overcoming problems helps make people stronger individuals? Why or why not?

Extension Activities

Reading Prompt ● Using Questioning in Research

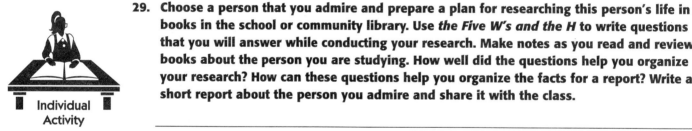

29. Choose a person that you admire and prepare a plan for researching this person's life in books in the school or community library. Use _the Five W's and the H_ to write questions that you will answer while conducting your research. Make notes as you read and review books about the person you are studying. How well did the questions help you organize your research? How can these questions help you organize the facts for a report? Write a short report about the person you admire and share it with the class.

Individual
Activity

_____

_____

_____

_____

_____

_____

_____

_____

_____

_____

150 Language Arts

Lesson 6

Cooperative Group Activity

Viewing Prompt ● Conducting an Interview

30. **Work with a group. Each member should choose a favorite character from a movie. Jot down facts about the character you choose, and pretend to be this character. All the members will play their characters and interview each other. Use *the 5 W's and the H* to make a list of questions you will ask in the interview. Take turns asking each other questions about the characters they are portraying. Do not mention the name of the character you are portraying in your answers. After the interviews are over, see how many characters you can identify from the answers to *the 5 W's and the H*.**

_____

_____

_____

_____

_____

_____

_____

_____

_____

Writing Prompt ● Using Problem-Solving Skills

Workplace Readiness Activity

31. **Work with a group. Research the work of a marketing specialist. How do these people help businesses find ways of increasing sales? What kinds of projects have marketers used successfully? What kinds of companies use contests and drawings as sales and marketing tools? Talk about ways in which *the 5 W's and the H* can be used by marketers in identifying the people they wish to reach with their marketing plans. How can the questioning process be used to learn more about careers in marketing? Research these careers and write a group report about them. Share your report with the class.**

_____

_____

_____

_____

_____

_____

_____

_____

_____

Classroom Discussion

What do you do when you come to an unfamiliar word in a book you're reading? What steps can you take to figure out the meaning? How can you add new words to your vocabulary every week?

Classroom Activity

Read the material below. Then follow the steps and answer the questions in the boxes.

To find the meaning of an unfamiliar word, you can use one of two methods. You can look up the word in a dictionary. There you can find out how to pronounce the word, what part of speech it is, and all of its possible meanings. Another way is to use **context clues**. That means looking at the words and sentences around the unfamiliar word. "Context" means how a word is used in a particular case. By reading the words around the unfamiliar word, you can find out what part of speech it is and even guess what it means. To check if your guess makes sense, replace the unfamiliar word with the meaning you guessed. You can use a dictionary to see if your guess was correct.

Poetry can sometimes seem hard to understand. You may come across several unfamiliar words in a single poem. But if you read the poem carefully and think about what the poet is trying to say, you can figure out the meaning. Think about how the words fit together. Look for context clues to each unfamiliar word. Try to understand the overall meaning of the poem.

Read the first part of this poem by Percy Bysshe Shelley (1792-1822). The title, "Ozymandias," is a form of the name for Ramses II, a famous Egyptian king. Look for the word in bold type. Think about the poem's meaning as you read.

Ozymandias

I met a traveler from an antique land

Who said: "Two vast and trunkless legs of stone

Stand in the desert. . . . Near them, on the sand,

Half sunk, a shattered **visage** lies, whose frown,

And wrinkled lip, and sneer of cold command

Tell that its sculptor well those passions read

Which yet survive, stamped on these lifeless things,

The hand that mocked them, and the heart that fed;

And on the pedestal these words appear;

'My name is Ozymandias, king of kings;

Look on my works, ye Mighty, and despair!'

Nothing beside remains. Round the decay

Of that colossal wreck, boundless and bare

The lone and level sands stretch far away.

Language Arts

Step 1

Look for context clues to find the meaning of an unfamiliar word.

1. **What is the unfamiliar word in bold type in the fourth line?**

   _____

2. **What part of speech is this word?**

   _____

3. **According to the poem, where is the visage?**

   _____

4. **Notice that the visage is the work of a sculptor. What do you think the visage is made of?**

   _____

5. **What else does the visage have?**

   _____

Step 2

Use context clues to guess the meaning of the word.

6. **What part of a statue has a frown and a wrinkled lip?**

   _____

7. **What do you think is the meaning of the word "visage"?**

   _____

Step 3

Use a dictionary to find the actual meaning of the word.

8. **In a dictionary, look up the word "visage." What does it mean?**

   _____

Step 4

Analyze the overall meaning of the poem.

9. **Whose visage is lying in the desert sand?**

   _____

10. **What kind of person was this?**

    _____

11. **What has happened to the statue of this person?**

    _____

12. In your own words, what does this poem mean?

_____

_____

_____

Open-Ended Question

13. Think about your answer to this question. Write your answer on the lines. Be prepared to talk about your answer in a classroom discussion. In England, there are statues and monuments that honor the great poet Percy Bysshe Shelley. Judging by his poem "Ozymandias," what would Shelley have thought about these monuments?

_____

_____

_____

_____

_____

Ideas to Remember

context clues—the words and sentences around an unfamiliar word
that can be used to guess the meaning of the word

Guided Practice Activity

Read the following poem. Look for the unfamiliar words in bold type. Then fill in the chart below.

He Had His Dream

He had his dream, and all through life,

Worked up to it through toil and **strife**.

Afloat fore'er before his eyes,

It colored for him all his skies:

　　The storm-cloud dark

　　Above his bark,

The calm and listless vault of blue

Took on its hopeful hue,

It **tinctured** every passing beam —

　　He had his dream.

Language Arts

He labored hard and failed at last,

His sails too weak to bear the blast,

The raging **tempests** tore away

And sent his beating bark astray.

But what cared he

For wind or sea!

He said, "The tempest will be short,

My bark will come to port."

He saw through every cloud a gleam —

He had his dream.

— Paul Laurence Dunbar (1872-1906)

14. Unfamiliar word: _____

   Context clues to the word's meaning: _____

   _____

   Part of speech: _____

   Your guess of the word's meaning: _____

   Dictionary meaning of the word: _____

15. Unfamiliar word: _____

   Context clues to the word's meaning: _____

   _____

   Part of speech: _____

   Your guess of the word's meaning: _____

   Dictionary meaning of the word: _____

16. Unfamiliar word: _____

   Context clues to the word's meaning: _____

   _____

   Part of speech: _____

   Your guess of the word's meaning: _____

   Dictionary meaning of the word: _____

17. In your own words, tell what this poem means.

_____

_____

_____

_____

Application Activity

Read the following poem. Look for the unfamiliar words in bold type. Then answer the questions that follow.

The Noiseless Patient Spider

A noiseless patient spider,

I mark'd where on a little **promontory** it stood isolated,

Mark'd how to explore the vacant vast surrounding,

It launched forth **filament**, filament, filament, out of itself,

Ever unreeling them, ever tirelessly speeding them.

And you O my soul where you stand,

Surrounded, detached, in measureless oceans of space,

Ceaselessly musing, venturing, throwing, seeking the spheres to connect them,

Till the bridge you will need be form'd, till the ductile anchor hold,

Till the **gossamer** thread you fling catch somewhere, O my soul.

— *Walt Whitman (1819-1892)*

Circle the letter of the correct answer to each question.

18. Where does the spider stand?

    a. in a crowd   c. in a spot by itself

    b. in a lonely spot   d. in a corner

19. From context clues, what do you think a *promontory* is?

    a. a branch of a tree   c. a telephone wire

    b. an isolated spot that overlooks something   d. a roof on a birdhouse

Language Arts

20. What part of speech is the word *filament*?

a. noun

b. verb

c. adjective

d. adverb

21. Where does the filament come from?

a. from the sky

b. from a leaf

c. from out of the spider

d. from the ground

22. How does the poet describe the filaments' movement?

a. They unreel.

b. They unravel.

c. They explode.

d. They curl.

23. From context clues, what do you think a filament is?

a. spider blood

b. beams of light

c. poison

d. strands of a spider web

24. What part of speech is the word *gossamer*?

a. noun

b. verb

c. adjective

d. adverb

25. What word does *gossamer* modify, or tell about?

a. bridge

b. anchor

c. spider

d. thread

26. Think about the size and texture of a spider's web. From context clues, what do you think *gossamer* means?

a. light, thin, and delicate

b. heavy and sturdy

c. thick and black

d. curly and sticky

Open-Ended Question

27. Use a separate piece of paper or write in your literary response journal. Refer to the information in this lesson.

Carefully reread the poem "A Noiseless Patient Spider."

- Why do you think Whitman repeats the word "filament" three times in the fourth line?

- How does the poet compare himself to the spider?

Extension Activities

Viewing Prompt ● Noting Unfamiliar Words in Television Shows

Individual Activity

28. Watch a television program dealing with some special skill such as cooking, home repair, playing a sport, or creating handicrafts. Take notes on unfamiliar words in the program. Write down any context clues that would help you guess the meaning. After the program, look over your list of words and context clues and make guesses as to the meaning of each word. Use a dictionary to see if your guesses were correct. Write a sentence using each word. Be prepared to explain how each word is used as a part of the special skill shown on the program.

_____

_____

_____

Reading Prompt ● Decoding the Work of Contemporary Poets

Cooperative Group Activity

29. Work with a partner. Go to the library and find a book of poems by a contemporary American poet such as Rita Dove or Maya Angelou. Take turns reading a poem aloud. Make note of any unfamiliar words and try to guess their meanings using context clues. After one of you reads a poem, have the other partner paraphrase its meaning. Discuss each poem and decide which poems you like best and why. Read two or three of your favorite poems to the rest of the class and lead a discussion about their meanings.

_____

_____

_____

Speaking Prompt ● Evaluate Information for Completeness

Workplace Readiness Activity

30. Work with a group. Discuss how technical manuals often feature words and terms that are unfamiliar to the average person. Bring up the following questions for discussion: How should a person find out the meanings of these words? Why is it important to understand the exact meaning? Should the meaning be included in the manual? What problems could occur if the reader doesn't understand the correct meaning? Have each member of the group bring an owner's manual for some appliance or other mechanical household device such as a CD player or string lawn trimmer. Divide into smaller groups and have each group examine one of the manuals closely. Write down any unfamiliar words and terms and include the context clues you find. Make guesses about the words' meanings and use a dictionary to check your work. When you gather again with the larger group, talk about the language in the manuals. Were the booklets easy to read and understand? Was it necessary to have a dictionary in order to use the manual? How could the manual you examined be improved?

_____

_____

_____

Language Arts

Classroom
Discussion

What is the difference between having a feeling or belief about something and putting bits of information together to reach a logical answer? Can an opinion be proved? Why or why not? Can a conclusion be proved? Why or why not?

Classroom
Activity

Details often are like clues that help you understand what you read or hear. Being able to select and use the most important clues can help you understand what you are hearing or reading.

Read and examine the information below. Then answer the questions that follow.

As people listen to speeches or broadcasts, they think about what they hear, and they make decisions about it. They either form opinions, or they draw conclusions. An **opinion** is what a writer, speaker, reader, or listener thinks about a topic. Opinions cannot be proved. Opinions are often formed with emotions. When people decide whether they like something or not, they are allowing their emotions to help determine what they think. People often disagree with each other's opinions. When people **draw conclusions**, they examine facts and then make a determination about what might have happened or what the facts mean when they are combined. People who solve mysteries draw conclusions by putting clues together to determine what happened. Whether you draw conclusions or form opinions, you should always examine the facts before doing so. Examine the facts in the article below.

Born in 1887, Georgia O'Keeffe began taking art lessons in 1898 at age eleven. By age twelve, she had determined that she would be an artist. At a time when women were thought to belong only in the home, O'Keeffe wanted to draw and paint, and she wanted to study how to do it well. Her family moved from Wisconsin to Virginia, where Georgia went to boarding school. From boarding school, she went to Chicago to study at the world-famous Art Institute of Chicago. The Art Institute is still the best school of art in the world. She spent a year in Chicago and then moved on to New York, where she studied at the Art Students League. While an art student in Chicago, O'Keeffe became friends with a fellow student, Anita Pollitzer. After the year in Chicago, the two women students began writing each other regularly.

Pollitzer stayed in New York, while O'Keeffe went back to Chicago to work as a commercial artist. She went on to study with a famous art teacher at the University of Virginia, who taught her to invent her own forms instead of trying to duplicate what had been accepted in the past. From there, O'Keeffe took several jobs teaching art in Virginia, South Carolina, and Texas, where she fell in love with the landscape of the southwestern United States. All the while, she was becoming better at expressing her thoughts and feelings in her art. Meanwhile, she had sent her friend Anita Pollitzer some black-and-white drawings that she had done. Pollitzer thought they were so good that she took them to a photography shop that had art exhibits from time to time. The shop was owned by a man named Alfred Stiegletz. Not only was he a photographer, he was an art critic. He loved O'Keeffe's drawings and, after a time, asked Pollitzer to introduce him to O'Keeffe.

GO TO NEXT PAGE

Lesson 8

Step 1

Look for the central ideas in the article.

1. **What is the central idea of the first paragraph?**

_____

2. **What is the central idea of the second paragraph?**

_____

_____

Step 2

Look for facts and details that support the central idea.

3. **What details and facts support the central idea in the first paragraph?**

_____

_____

_____

4. **What details and facts support the central idea in the second paragraph?**

_____

_____

_____

_____

Step 3

Locate facts and details to determine the writer's opinions.

5. **What opinion does the writer express in the first paragraph?**

_____

6. **What is the writer's opinion about Georgia O'Keeffe as an artist? How can you tell?**

_____

_____

_____

Language Arts

Step 4

Use the facts and details to form your own opinions.

7. From what you have read in this article, what kind of artist do you think Georgia O'Keeffe was?

_____

8. What facts and details helped you form your opinion?

_____

_____

Open-Ended Question

9. Think about your answer to the following question. Write your answer on the lines. Be prepared to talk about your answer in a classroom discussion. Georgia O'Keeffe loved a mountain named the Pedernal that she could see from her window. To explain why the mountain appears in so many of her paintings, O'Keeffe once said, "God told me if I painted that mountain enough, He would give it to me." What do you think she meant by that statement?

_____

_____

_____

_____

_____

_____

_____

_____

_____

_____

Ideas to Remember

opinion–what someone believes to be right or prefers

drawing conclusions–using the facts and details in a story to figure out what is happening, what the characters are like, or what the outcome will be

Guided Practice Activity

Read the following paragraphs. Then follow the steps and answer the questions.

Alfred Stieglitz was so taken with the drawings that Georgia O'Keeffe had done that he asked Anita Pollitzer if he could read her letters. Then Georgia began writing directly to him, asking for his thoughts about her work. Georgia began to teach at Columbia University in New York. Without her knowledge, Stieglitz arranged to show several of her drawings in his shop, 291. Upon learning about the show, she marched into the shop and demanded that he remove the drawings from the wall. Stieglitz refused, and the show continued. This show helped the public realize that women could be artists, as well as men. O'Keeffe's art helped to push women into the spotlight as artists and caused people to take their art seriously. O'Keeffe is the greatest woman artist of the century. Georgia again took a job outside New York teaching art, but Stieglitz was so impressed with her talent that he sent a representative from his shop to bring her back to New York for a year. He promised to pay all her expenses if she would live in New York and paint. O'Keeffe agreed, and it wasn't long before the two had plans to marry.

Stieglitz began to act as O'Keeffe's agent. He showed her paintings and introduced her to other well-known artists and critics. Georgia helped Stieglitz with his photography and allowed him to photograph her for a collection he was creating on women. He wanted to show women not as wearing fancy ball gowns and jewels, but as they were in their homes while cooking, washing, and caring for children. He wanted to photograph real women. Women in ball gowns and heavy jewelry are boring, and no one cares about them. Each of them helped to enhance the other's chosen art form.

Step 1

Look for the central ideas in the article.

10. What is the central idea in the first paragraph?

_____

11. What is the central idea of the second paragraph?

_____

Step 2

Look for facts and details that support the central idea.

12. What details support the central idea in the first paragraph?

_____

_____

_____

_____

_____

Language Arts

13. What details support the central idea in the second paragraph?

_____

_____

_____

_____

Step 3

Locate facts and details to determine the writer's or speaker's opinions.

14. What opinions does the writer express in each paragraph?

_____

_____

_____

Step 4

Use the facts and details to form your own opinions.

15. How important do you consider the work of Georgia O'Keeffe to be in the world of modern art? Why?

_____

_____

_____

Application Activity

Read the information below. Then answer the questions that follow.

For many years, Georgia O'Keeffe lived her life in New York in the role of the wife of Alfred Stieglitz. She went to Lake George with him to spend summers with his family. During cold weather she lived on the top floor of an apartment building with him. Stieglitz continued to represent O'Keeffe as her agent and to sell her paintings. The two were inseparable even though his large, noisy family at times made Georgia uneasy. But through the years, Alfred Stieglitz grew old and ill-tempered. He often complained of illnesses, and he turned his attention to a much younger woman. For a few years, O'Keeffe stayed to take care of him, but eventually she grew ill herself from the strain. She longed to see the West and her beloved landscapes again. She decided to go to New Mexico for a summer to visit friends and regain her strength.

While Georgia was in Taos, New Mexico for the summer, she began to paint again. She became interested in the symbols and the sweeping landscapes of New Mexico. She participated in the culture of the area and visited pueblos. She painted the hills and mesas of New Mexico, as well as the crimson-red sky of sunset. By the time she returned to New York, she took crates of newly created paintings with her. While in New York, she had painted huge flowers. She turned the immensity around to focus on the grandness of the New Mexican landscape.

GO TO NEXT PAGE

In 1930 O'Keeffe prepared to return to New Mexico for the summer. She asked Stieglitz to go with her. However, he had been out of the New York area only once in his life, and he saw no reason why people should want to travel and see the world. However, she felt that in order to continue painting, she would have to get out of the city and away from the many illnesses of Stieglitz, some of them imagined. She began spending every summer in New Mexico with friends. In 1940, she bought her own home in New Mexico's Ghost Ranch region. She continued spending her summers in New Mexico and returning to New York in the winter to live with Stieglitz. Her paintings brought her fame as an artist and eventually made her wealthy. Then, in 1946, Stieglitz died. Georgia spent three years in New York settling his estate. After that, she closed up their home in New York and moved to New Mexico to stay. She loved the brilliant colors of the landscape, even though the climate could be harsh. She thought that New Mexico was the most beautiful place on Earth. Everyone who visits there comes away with the feeling that its beauty is unsurpassed anywhere.

At age sixty-three, O'Keeffe began traveling on other continents. She moved from country to country absorbing nature and its structure, as well as the structure of all the marvelous things made by humans. Her travels gave her countless subjects for her paintings. Her art was exhibited in several of the world's most important art galleries and museums.

O'Keeffe returned to her beloved New Mexico and continued to paint and live in her isolated adobe home in the country. She worked until she was in her eighties, when she became almost blind. The subjects of her paintings changed from time to time, going from skyscrapers to giant flowers to barns, shells, and the landscape of New Mexico. She selected her subjects according to where she was at the time. Her art has been on exhibit perhaps more than that of any other woman artist, and she is highly respected and revered for her enormous talent and her perseverance to create. O'Keeffe was overtaken by old age and died in 1985 at the age of ninety-eight. She will long be remembered for her devotion to her art, for her tremendous talent, and for her willingness to give up many of life's comforts in order to create what seemed most natural to her.

16. What is the central idea of the first paragraph? Circle the letter of your answer.

a. The constant noise made by the Stieglitz family usually embarrassed O'Keeffe and made her uncomfortable.

b. O'Keeffe spent all her time with Stieglitz and his family even though it eventually made her health suffer.

c. O'Keeffe disliked moving from the apartment to the country and back again, but she did it because she loved Stieglitz.

17. What is the central idea of the third paragraph? Circle the letter of your answer.

a. Stieglitz was selfish because he tried to keep O'Keeffe from going to New Mexico to paint.

b. O'Keeffe loved the harshness of the New Mexican climate, and she could hardly wait to go there to feel the hot wind on her face.

c. O'Keeffe felt that she had to go to New Mexico to continue painting, and so she went without Stieglitz.

Language Arts

18. What is the central idea of the entire selection? Circle the letter of your answer.

    a. O'Keeffe was selfish not to want to stay with Stieglitz even though she felt that she must create art.

    b. O'Keeffe's main goal was to express herself and what she saw in her art, and she was one of the best women artists in the world.

    c. O'Keeffe fell in love with the New Mexico desert and wanted to be there, even if she had to give up everthing else she loved, including her art.

19. What are some facts and details that support the central idea?

_____

_____

20. What is the writer's opinion about O'Keeffe and her accomplishments?

_____

_____

21. What opinion about New Mexico is expressed in this selection?

_____

_____

22. Why does this opinion not belong in the selection?

_____

_____

23. What are some facts and details that support the writer's opinion about Georgia O'Keefe and her work?

_____

_____

_____

Open-Ended Question

24. Use a separate piece of paper or write in your literary response journal. Refer to the information in the Application Activity.

● Was it appropriate for O'Keeffe to have given up time with her aging and sick husband to go to New Mexico so that she could continue to paint?

● What sacrifices do artists have to make to become successful?

Extension Activities

Listening Prompt ● Listening for Opinions

25. **Listen to television commercials. How many opinions do you hear in every commercial? Write down the opinions that you hear in commercials for one evening. Share your findings with the class.**

_____

_____

_____

_____

_____

_____

Individual Activity

Viewing Prompt ● Reviewing a News Magazine Broadcast

26. **Work with a group. Select a news magazine broadcast such as _Dateline_, _Sixty Minutes_, or _Time and Again_ and watch one episode. Determine which statements were conclusions drawn from information gathered by the staff and which are opinions of someone on the staff. As you record these statements, make notes about why you think each statement is either a conclusion or an opinion.**

_____

_____

_____

_____

_____

Cooperative Group Activity

Speaking Prompt ● Determining Job Qualifications

27. **Work with a group. Acquire the qualifications list for several jobs that are available at the present time. Determine whether the qualifications are actually necessary for someone to do the job well, or whether each qualification is someone's opinion of what should be necessary for employment. Present your findings to the class orally.**

_____

_____

_____

_____

Workplace Readiness Activity

Language Arts

Interpretations of Conventions of
Print and Speech

Classroom Discussion

What kind of weather is it when it feels "like an oven outside"? What other comparisons do you make to describe different kinds of weather? Have you heard people say a car is "stubborn" when it won't start? What kind of figure of speech is that?

Classroom Activity

Read the material below. Then answer the questions in the boxes.

Just like any craftsperson, poets use tools in their work. These tools include figures of speech and structural tools. Figures of speech are used to compare things and create images. Structural tools are used to build the poem and give it a certain form.

Figures of Speech		
Name	**What It Does**	**Example**
Simile	compares two unlike things using the words "like" or "as"	The pond at night reflected the moon like a black mirror.
Metaphor	compares two unlike things directly	The pond was a black mirror reflecting the white moon.
Personification	assigns human qualities to nonhuman things	The old couch let out a groan as my cousin plopped down on its cushions.
Structural Tools		
Name	**What It Is**	**Example**
Rhyme	placing words that have the same ending sound at the end of lines	I love the *shapes* Of pears and *grapes*.
Meter	using the same rhythm for each line	Be*neath* the *cloud*less *skies* The *ship* set *sail* for *home*.
Stanza	dividing the lines of a poem into groups	Deep within a garden A single droning bee Makes circles in a sunbeam. He touches down at last Upon the trembling petal Of summer's last white rose.

Read the following poem. Then follow the steps and answer the questions.

Almost Breakfast

A bluejay bobs its beak and gropes
For early worms in the tall wet grass.
It twitches more the more it hopes
To snare its breakfast with one good pass.

Hopping with joy, it spies its prey
Looped like a rope around a root.
But before the jay can have its way
Its meal is crushed by the gardener's boot.

Step 1

Look for examples of simile and metaphor.

1. **What is the difference between a simile and a metaphor?**

   _____

   _____

2. **Look at the comparison in the sixth line of the poem "Almost Breakfast." Is this a simile or a metaphor? Why?**

   _____

3. **What two things are being compared?**

   _____

Step 2

Look for examples of personification.

4. **What is personification?**

   _____

5. **What does the bluejay do in the fifth line of the poem?**

   _____

6. **Why is this an example of personification?**

   _____

 Language Arts

Step 3

Look for the effects of rhyme, meter, and spacing on the page.

7. Does this poem have a regular rhythm or meter? If so, how many stresses are in each line?

_____

8. What is a stanza used to do?

_____

9. How many stanzas does this poem have?

_____

10. How many lines are in each stanza?

_____

11. What are all the pairs of rhyming words in this poem?

_____

Open-Ended Question

12. Think about your answers to these questions. Write your answers on the lines. Be prepared to talk about your answers in a classroom discussion. How did you react when you read the last line of the poem? Why is it a surprise?

_____

_____

_____

_____

_____

_____

_____

_____

Ideas to Remember

rhyme–words that have the same ending sound at the end of the lines in a poem

meter–the regular rhythm of a line of poetry

stanza–a group of lines in a poem that usually recur in the same number and pattern

Guided Practice Activity

Read the following poems. Then answer the questions.

"Let It Be Forgotten"

Let it be forgotten, as a flower is forgotten,
    Forgotten as a fire that once was singing gold.
Let it be forgotten for ever and ever —
    Time is a kind friend, he will make us old.

If anyone asks, say it was forgotten
    Long and long ago —
As a flower, as a fire, as a hushed footfall
    In a long forgotten snow.

               — *Sara Teasdale (1884-1933)*

A Forgotten House

No one is worried anymore
about the broken windows,
the missing boards in the porch
like gaps in a loved one's memory, the torn
screens, the fallen
shingles, the grass
so long uncut, or how
the roof has contracted a slouch.
Once there were children's voices
raised in play, but now
even the sign in the yard
is silent, too choked by grass
to murmur "For Sale."

13. What metaphor is in the first poem?

_____

14. Does the second poem contain a simile or a metaphor? Name it.

_____

15. What lines in the second poem contain personification?

_____

16. What thing is being described as if it were a person?

_____

17. Which of the two poems is written in stanzas?

_____

18. How many lines are in each stanza?

_____

19. Which poem includes lines that rhyme? Write the pairs of rhyming words.

_____

20. Which poem is written in meter, or in lines that have a rhythm that repeats?

_____

Application
Activity

Read the poems. Look for the tools and forms of poetry that you've learned in this lesson. Then answer the questions that follow.

The Plan

In slow, slow loops
sketched high against the clouds
like a speck moving on clean white paper,
a hawk makes preparations —
for what?

Her loops are her thoughts.
She ponders in slow circles
until, with the speed of a sudden decision,
she sails down a long curved slide of air
and executes the plan.

The Eagle

He clasps the crag with crooked hands,

Close to the sun in lonely lands,

Ringed with the azure world, he stands.

The wrinkled sea beneath him crawls,

He watches from his mountain walls,

And like a thunderbolt he falls.

— *Alfred, Lord Tennyson (1809-1892)*

Read each question and circle the letter of the correct answer.

21. **In the first poem, the words "like a speck moving on clean white paper" is an example of what?**
    a. simile   c. meter
    b. metaphor   d. personification

22. **Which of the following lines contains a metaphor?**
    a. In slow, slow loops   c. Her loops are her thoughts
    b. a hawk makes preparations   d. and executes the plan

23. **How many stanzas are there in the first poem?**
    a. 1   c. 3
    b. 2   d. 4

24. **What is personified, or given human qualities, in the first poem?**
    a. the loops   c. the hawk
    b. the cloud   d. the slide

25. **What is the simile in the second poem?**
    a. He clasps the crag   c. The wrinkled sea beneath him crawls
    b. Ringed with the azure world   d. like a thunderbolt

26. **Which tool of poetry is NOT used in the poem "The Eagle"?**
    a. metaphor   c. meter
    b. rhyme   d. stanza

27. **What is the meaning of the word "crag" in line one of "The Eagle"?**
    a. a steep rock   c. a thick root
    b. a tree limb   d. a steel bar

                    Language Arts

Open-Ended Question

28. Use a separate piece of paper or write in your literary response journal. Refer to the information in this lesson.

Reread the poems "The Plan" and "The Eagle."

● How are these poems alike and different?

● Why do you think the writer of "The Plan" chose the word "executes" in the last line? Does it have a double meaning?

Extension Activities

Writing Prompt ● Using the Tools of Poetry

Individual Activity

29. **Study the poems in this lesson and how they make use of the tools of poetry. Then write your own poem, using as many of these tools as you can. To write in meter, try to employ the same rhythm for each line of your poem. In using rhyme, remember that the rhymes can follow a certain pattern or be used freely to link certain lines. Try to make your poem sound natural and fluid, as if you were speaking to someone. Be original in your comparisons when you use metaphors and similes. When you've finished your poem, read it to another student or a group of students. See if they can name all the tools of poetry that you used. Discuss the meaning of your poem and how you used the form of the poem to achieve that meaning.**

Listening Prompt ● Identifying the Tools of Poetry in Song Lyrics

Cooperative Group Activity

30. **Work with a partner or small group. As you listen to your favorite songs on the radio or on a CD, write down the lyrics in the form of a poem. Do the lines divide naturally into groups or stanzas? What examples of simile, metaphor, and personification do you find? Do the lines rhyme and have a rhythm that repeats? Analyze the lyrics of several songs and make a chart to show what tools of poetry are included in each.**

Speaking Prompt ● Using the Library Media Center as a Critical Resource

Workplace Readiness Activity

31. **Work with a group. Prepare a list of poets to study, such as Maya Angelou, Derek Walcott, Amy Clampitt, Richard Wilbur, and Rita Dove. Look in the library media center, both on the shelves and online, to find poems by these writers and information about their backgrounds, lives, and work. When you have compiled a biography of each poet, discuss them. What kinds of work do these writers do to support their poetry? Why might it be difficult to make a living as a full-time poet? How could a poet use his or her skills in other areas to make money? How might a poet find ways to introduce poetry to people who don't ordinarily read it? Discuss why it is important to have poets in a society. Ask members of the group if they would like to become professional poets themselves.**

Classroom Discussion

What do you concentrate on when you listen to someone make a speech? Do you pay closer attention to a speaker with whom you agree? How do you compare the speaker's point of view with your own?

Classroom Activity

To understand a speech it helps to understand its purpose. A speech can have the following purposes.

Purpose of Speech	Example
Inform	a lecture on American history delivered by a college professor
Entertain	a humorous speech about childhood delivered by a well-known writer
Persuade	a campaign speech by a candidate for President
Instruct	a talk on how to grow fruit trees delivered by an expert in horticulture

As you listen to a speech, note the major points made by the speaker. Try to determine the speaker's point of view and compare it to your own. Think of questions you'd like to ask when the speech is over. By being an active listener, you will get more out of the speech.

The following excerpt is from John F. Kennedy's inaugural address as President of the United States. It was delivered on the steps of the Capitol building in Washington, D.C. on January 20, 1961. Read it silently or read it aloud with a partner. Then follow the steps and answer the questions.

Let every nation know, whether it wishes us well or ill, that we shall pay any price, bear any burden, meet any hardship, support any friend, oppose any foe to assure the survival and the success of liberty.

This much we pledge—and more.

To those old allies whose cultural and spiritual origins we share, we pledge the loyalty of faithful friends. United, there is little we cannot do in a host of cooperative ventures. Divided, there is little we can do—for we dare not meet a powerful challenge at odds and split asunder.

To those new states whom we welcome to the ranks of the free, we pledge our word that one form of colonial control shall not have passed away merely to be replaced by a far more iron tyranny. We shall not always expect to find them supporting our view. But we shall always hope to find them strongly supporting their own freedom—and to remember that, in the past, those who foolishly sought power by riding the back of the tiger ended up inside.

GO TO NEXT PAGE

To those peoples in the huts and villages of half the globe struggling to break the bonds of mass misery, we pledge our best efforts to help them help themselves, for whatever period is required—not because the Communists may be doing it, not because we seek their votes, but because it is right. If a free society cannot help the many who are poor, it cannot save the few who are rich.

. . . Finally, to those nations who would make themselves our adversary, we offer not a pledge but a request: that both sides begin anew the quest for peace, before the dark powers of destruction unleashed by science engulf all humanity in planned or accidental self-destruction.

We dare not tempt them with weakness. For only when our arms are sufficient beyond doubt can we be certain beyond doubt that they will never be employed.

. . . In your hands, my fellow citizens, more than mine, will rest the final success or failure of our course. Since this country was founded, each generation of Americans has been summoned to give testimony to its national loyalty. The graves of young Americans who answered the call to service surround the globe.

. . . In the long history of the world, only a few generations have been granted the role of defending freedom in its hour of maximum danger. I do not shrink from this responsibility — I welcome it. I do not believe that any of us would exchange places with any other people or any other generation. The energy, the faith, the devotion which we bring to this endeavor will light our country and all who serve it—and the glow from that fire can truly light the world.

And so, my fellow Americans: ask not what your country can do for you—ask what you can do for your country.

Step 1

Identify the topic of the speech.

1. What was the occasion for this speech?

_____

2. What is President Kennedy's topic in this speech?

_____

_____

_____

Step 2

Identify the purpose of the speech.

3. As the new president, what did Kennedy want to tell his audience?

_____

_____

4. Who was President Kennedy's audience for this speech?

_____

GO TO NEXT PAGE

5. **Is the main purpose of this speech to inform, entertain, persuade, or instruct?**

_____

_____

Step 3

Note the main points of the speech.

6. **What did Kennedy want to tell each of the following groups?**

Old allies: _____

_____

New states: _____

_____

Peoples in the huts and villages: _____

_____

Nations who would be enemies of the United States: _____

_____

7. **What qualities does Kennedy say the new generation of Americans has that will help them in the struggle for liberty?**

_____

_____

8. **Reread the last paragraph. Why is it an important part of the speech?**

_____

_____

_____

_____

_____

_____

Language Arts

Step 4

Think of important questions about the speech.

9. Read the following questions about President Kennedy's speech. Place an X beside each question that covers an important point in the speech.

____ How will the U.S. government help poor people in other countries?

____ How often will President Kennedy travel to other countries?

____ How can the U.S. and its enemies work together to prevent a destructive war?

____ Does President Kennedy believe that Americans in the past have been selfish in thinking only about what the government could do for them?

____ Does President Kennedy plan to make any changes to the floorplan of the White House?

Open-Ended Question

10. Think about your answer to the following question. Write your answer on the lines. Be prepared to talk about your answer in a classroom discussion. Pretend you are a reporter covering President Kennedy's inaugural address. How would you summarize his speech in a short paragraph?

_____

_____

_____

_____

_____

_____

_____

_____

_____

_____

_____

_____

_____

_____

Ideas to Remember

speaker's purpose–the reasons for making a speech; to inform, entertain, persuade, or instruct

Lesson 10

Guided Practice Activity

Read the following short speech. Then answer the questions that follow.

Most of Shakespeare's greatest plays were first performed at the Globe, a theater in London, England. Before theaters like the Globe were built, actors performed plays wherever they could. This included at fairs, in the courtyards of inns, and occasionally at great houses or at court. Having a theater building of their own gave acting companies greater freedom to create their plays.

Built in 1599, the Globe was very different from theaters of today. Plays were done in the open air, with the audience seated very close to the stage. Performances began at two in the afternoon. Vendors sold food and drinks to the playgoers. Seats were purchased by well-to-do people, while others, called the groundlings, crowded at the foot of the stage. The building itself had three levels, with the stage jutting from the back wall into the center area. A roof covered the seats and part of the stage. Actors would enter the stage area through doors at the side. Some scenes took place aloft, to represent a tower or the walls of a city. There was very little scenery or props; perhaps a table for a banquet scene or a chair to represent a king's throne. Costumes, however, were quite elaborate. There was no curtain in front of the stage. The actors stepped on and off the stage in full view of the audience. The scenes of a play unfolded in rapid order. To help the audience, actors often announced the setting of a scene in their lines. As simple as the Globe was, its productions were a popular attraction. Audiences would sit enthralled by the balcony scene between Romeo and Juliet or would wildly cheer King Henry V's victory on the battlefield.

Step 1

Identify the topic of the speech.

11. What is the topic of this speech?

_____

12. What sort of person would deliver a speech like this?

_____

Step 2

Identify the purpose of the speech.

13. Does this speech seek to inform, entertain, persuade, or instruct?

_____

14. Who do you think is the intended audience for this speech?

_____

_____

15. Where would a speech like this be delivered?

_____

 Language Arts

Step 3

Note the main points of the speech.

16. What was the Globe?

_____

17. Before theaters like the Globe were built, where did acting companies perform plays?

_____

18. How was the Globe different from theaters of our time?

_____

_____

_____

_____

Step 4

Think of important questions about the speech.

19. Write three questions you would like to ask this speaker about the topic.

_____

_____

_____

_____

_____

_____

Application Activity

Read the following speech. Then answer the questions that follow.

City planners sometimes act as if they don't know what people want in a city. Their plans suggest that city people want emptiness, order, and silence above anything else. But why do most people live in cities? They love to see activity, they love to watch other people on the streets. Nothing brings joy to the heart of a city dweller like swirls of colorful activity—street fairs, outdoor cafes, ballgame crowds, museum goers, afternoon strollers, and the like. But city planners, with their walls and courtyards and tunnels, seem anxious to keep people apart rather than bring them together.

One obvious concern is safety. But which seems safer to you—a street crowded with a variety of people going about their daily business or a deserted street with one or two strangers lingering in doorways or alleyways? A lively street not only has lots of users, it has lots of "eyes" to watch out for trouble. Tenants who sit inside the walls of their house or apartment building don't help in this regard. Rather it's the shopkeepers and restaurant owners, the dog walkers and the joggers, the fruit stand vendors and the street musicians who keep an eye on the neighborhood. These people

GO TO NEXT PAGE

feel that they have a proprietary interest in the block; they *care about* what goes on there. Why don't city planners encourage the growth of these kinds of neighborhoods by widening sidewalks, adding benches, lights, and fountains, and luring people into the streets on foot rather than in automobiles? This would make our cities more colorful and interesting and make a walk in the afternoon as eventful as a parade.

20. What is the topic of this speech?
   a. how city planners can do a better job of designing cities
   b. why large cities are the best places to live
   c. why cities are dangerous
   d. how a city planner designs the neighborhoods of a city

21. What is the speaker's purpose in this speech?
   a. to inform
   b. to entertain
   c. to persuade
   d. to instruct

22. What changes would the speaker like to see to improve the design of cities?
   a. more emptiness, order, and silence
   b. more roadways for automobiles
   c. more open areas in neighborhoods to encourage activity on the streets
   d. more deserted streets where only one or two strangers can be seen

23. Which of the following would the speaker prefer to be used in city designs?
   a. walls and fences
   b. courtyards and high-rise apartments
   c. tunnels
   d. wider sidewalks and fountains

24. Why does the speaker think that a street filled with activity is safer than a deserted street?
   a. There are more police on patrol.
   b. There are more "eyes" of people in the neighborhood watching out for trouble.
   c. There is less crime in a neighborhood with lots of walls and tunnels.
   d. There is no room for criminals to operate in a crowded street.

25. Write three questions you would like to ask the speaker about this topic. Don't hesitate to express your own opinion in your questions.

_____

_____

_____

_____

_____

_____

_____

_____

 Language Arts

Open-Ended
Question

26. Use a separate piece of paper or write in your literary response journal. Refer to the information in the Application Activity.

● How would you improve the design of your city or town?

● How do you think the design of cities will be different 100 years from now?

Extension Activities

Listening Prompt ● Listening for a Speaker's Purpose

Individual
Activity

27. Listen to a speech at a school assembly or at some special event in your city. Take notes on the topic and supporting details. If possible, ask the speaker a question to follow up on the topic. Later, write down the speaker's purpose and tell how well that purpose was accomplished. Review your notes from the speech and write them in outline form. Then use them to write three more questions for the speaker, as if you were a reporter covering the speech.

_____

_____

_____

Speaking Prompt ● Creating a Speech Designed to Instruct

Cooperative
Group
Activity

28. Work with a partner. Each of you should choose a skill or task and describe how it is done in a short speech. Be sure to describe each step of the process in complete detail. After hearing your speech, the audience should be able to perform the skill or task just as you described it. When you're done, read your speech to your partner. Then listen to his or her speech. Discuss how well each of you described the skill or task. Were any steps left out or did any need to be described in more detail? What questions might the audience have after hearing your speech? Critique each other's work and use the comments to rewrite the speeches and improve them.

_____

_____

_____

Speaking Prompt ● Describe and Demonstrate Procedures for Basic First Aid

Workplace
Readiness
Activity

29. Work with a group. Discuss the importance of knowing first-aid techniques and why these skills are important in a work environment. Divide up into smaller groups and research a specific first-aid technique such as dealing with a cut or attending to someone who is choking. Work together to prepare a short speech describing this skill. Then gather again as a group and present short instructional speeches about basic first-aid skills. Be prepared to answer questions from the audience. Take notes on the other speeches so that you can ask questions yourself.

_____

_____

_____

Multiple Choice
Read the following questions and the four possible answers. Choose the answer to each question. Find the bubble next to the question that has the same letter as the answer you chose. Fill in this bubble to mark your answer.

Ⓐ Ⓑ Ⓒ Ⓓ   **1. What is the topic of a story or article?**
a. the details that give more information
b. the main idea that the author or speaker wants to present
c. the subject, or what the story or article tells about
d. the background of the story or article

Ⓐ Ⓑ Ⓒ Ⓓ   **2. What is the central idea of a story or article?**
a. the main point the author or speaker wants to present about the topic
b. the subject, or what the story or article tells about
c. the author or speaker's point of view
d. the middle part of the story or article

Ⓐ Ⓑ Ⓒ Ⓓ   **3. What does it mean to paraphrase a piece of writing?**
a. copy it word for word   c. rewrite it in your own words
b. analyze its meaning   d. translate it into another language

Ⓐ Ⓑ Ⓒ Ⓓ   **4. Which of the following is NOT an element of a fictional story?**
a. opening   c. setting
b. purpose   d. characters

Ⓐ Ⓑ Ⓒ Ⓓ   **5. What does an author or speaker do when he or she makes an audience laugh, feel sad, or experience suspense?**
a. inform   c. persuade
b. entertain   d. instruct

Ⓐ Ⓑ Ⓒ Ⓓ   **6. In the questioning procedure the Five W's and the H, what does H stand for?**
a. how?   c. how long ago?
b. home or away?   d. he or she?

Ⓐ Ⓑ Ⓒ Ⓓ   **7. What do you look at when you use context clues to determine the meaning of an unfamiliar word?**
a. the dictionary
b. the end of the story
c. the words and sentences around the unfamiliar word
d. the words of a character in the story

                    Language Arts

(A)(B)(C)(D) **8. What is an opinion?**
   a. what someone infers from hints and clues
   b. what someone believes to be right or prefers
   c. what someone finds out about a topic from a reference book
   d. what someone figures out from the details

(A)(B)(C)(D) **9. Which of the following describes a poem written in meter?**
   a. It has the same number of words in each line.
   b. It has the same basic rhythm in each line.
   c. It has groups of lines that repeat.
   d. It has rhyming words at the end of each line.

(A)(B)(C)(D) **10. What is the purpose of a campaign speech by a candidate for president?**
   a. inform   c. persuade
   b. entertain   d. instruct

Writing Prompt ● The Safety Song

Situation

You've been hired to write the lyrics for a song urging the public to drive more safely. Write your song lyrics as a poem.

Before You Write

As you prepare to write your poem, think about the following ideas:

● What is the topic and central idea of your poem?

● What is your purpose for writing the poem?

● What opinions will you include in the poem?

● What conclusions do you want your audience to draw?

● What tools of poetry will you use in your poem?

Write a poem to serve as the lyrics for a song about driving safety. You may write the poem in any style you wish. Be sure to think about your topic, main idea or theme, supporting details, opinions, and conclusions as you write. Complete your work on a separate piece of paper. You may wish to write in your literary response journal instead.

Speaking Prompt ● The Greatest Event in Your Childhood

Situation

As an international pop star, you're doing an interview with a reporter from the BBC. The interviewer has asked you to describe the single event from your childhood that is most memorable to you or had the greatest effect on your life.

Before You Speak

As you prepare your story, think about the following ideas:

● What are the topic, central idea, and supporting details for your story?

● What will be the opening, setting, events, and closing of your story?

● What purpose do you have in telling your story? How do you want your audience to react?

● What important points do you want to include in the story?

● What questions might the interviewer ask to follow up on the story?

With a partner, role-play an interview in which you answer the question about the greatest event in your childhood. Be prepared to answer follow-up questions from the interviewer. Note the basic ideas for your answer on a separate piece of paper. Be sure to include a topic, main idea or theme, supporting details, opinions, and conclusions. You can use such things as pictures, photographs, charts, diagrams, and note cards in your presentation. Speak clearly and confidently as you make your speech.

 Language Arts

**Classroom
Discussion**

**What can you tell about an event by examining a photograph of the action
that happened? How do pictures, photographs, charts, graphs, and other
visuals help viewers understand the point that the presenter is trying to make?**

**Classroom
Activity**

Look at the pictures below. Answer the questions that follow.

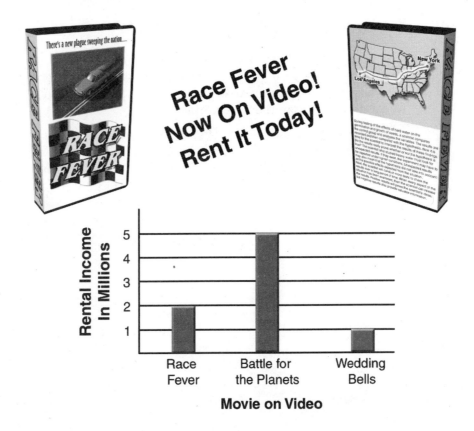

1. **Which picture shows an item that presents images and sounds for an audience to examine?**

   _____

2. **What kinds of events would you expect to see while viewing this item?**

   _____

3. **What can you learn about the race by examining the map shown on the package?**

   _____

4. **What kinds of numbers are presented on the graph?**

   _____

5. **According to the graph, which movie has been the most successful after being released
   on video?**

   _____

185

Lesson 1

Maps

Classroom Discussion

What ideas are shown on maps included in your history book? What ideas are shown on maps included in your science book? Why are maps effective tools in presenting certain kinds of information?

Classroom Activity

Read and examine the material below. Answer the questions in the boxes.

A **map** can show many kinds of details about one particular place or one main idea about the entire world. Even though maps may show different places and different ideas, they are prepared in similar ways. Knowing the basics about maps helps viewers understand any map they encounter.

A **map key**, sometimes known as a **legend**, is a list of symbols and explanations of what these symbols represent on the map. These symbols may be different kinds of lines that tell viewers which roads are city streets, which are highways, and which are under construction.

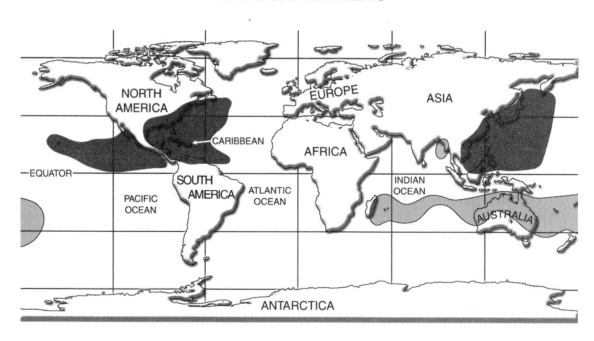

HURRICANE AREAS

Map Key

◼ Over 5 Hurricanes on Average Per Year
▨ Fewer than 5 Hurricanes on Average Per Year
☐ No Hurricanes

Language Arts

Lesson 1

Step 1

Study the elements that make up the map.

1. **What is the title of this map?**
   _____

2. **What part of the earth does this map show?**
   _____

3. **What do you think this map will show?**
   _____

4. **What is found printed beneath the map?**
   _____
   _____

Step 2

Identify the information contained in the map key.

5. **According to the map key, what does the dark color represent?**
   _____

6. **What does the medium color represent?**
   _____

7. **What do the white areas represent?**
   _____
   _____

Step 3

Make decisions about the information shown on the map.

8. **Which areas are likely to experience over 5 hurricanes per year?**
   _____
   _____
   _____

9. **What continent is likely to experience fewer than 5 hurricanes per year?**
   _____

10. **Are most land areas likely to experience hurricanes? Why or why not?**
    _____
    _____
    _____
    _____

Open-Ended
Question

11. Think about your answer to the following question. Write your answer on the lines. Be prepared to talk about your answer in a classroom discussion. Why is it important for scientists to identify where different kinds of storms are likely to hit each year?

_____

_____

_____

_____

_____

_____

_____

_____

_____

Ideas to
Remember

> **map key**–a guide that explains the symbols on a map, such as colors, lines, and shapes; also called a legend

Guided
Practice
Activity

Examine the map below. Then answer the questions.

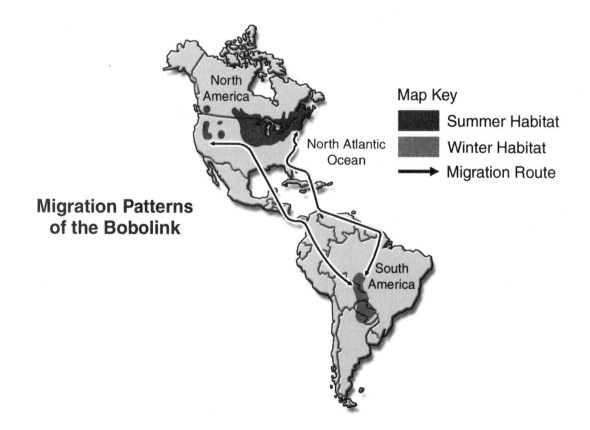

Migration Patterns of the Bobolink

Lesson 1

Step 1

Study the elements that make up the map.

12. **What is the title of this map?**

_____

13. **What part of the earth does this map show?**

_____

14. **What do you think this map will show?**

_____

15. **Where is the legend printed on this map?**

_____

Step 2

Identify the information contained in the map key.

16. **According to the map key, what does the first symbol represent?**

_____

17. **What does the second symbol represent?**

_____

18. **What does the last symbol represent?**

_____

Step 3

Make decisions about the information shown on the map.

19. **What continent is the location of the bobolink's summer habitat?**

_____

20. **What continent is the location of the bobolink's winter habitat?**

_____

21. **Which of these two habitats is larger?**

_____

22. **What kinds of areas does the bobolink cross on its migration route?**

_____

23. **During what season must the bobolink travel in order to reach its summer habitat?**

_____

24. **Look at the map. Does the bobolink travel north or south to reach its summer habitat?**

_____

25. **During what season and in what direction does the bobolink travel to reach its winter habitat?**

_____

Application Activity

Look at the map. Then answer the questions that follow.

U.S. Tornadoes of F4 Level or Higher Each 1,000 Years

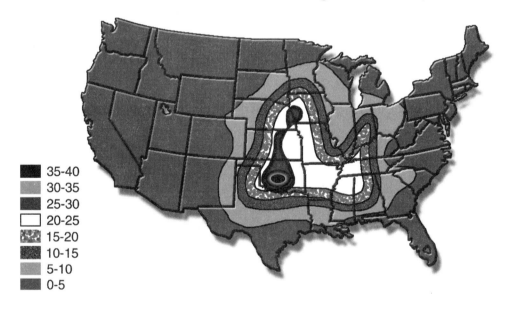

- 35-40
- 30-35
- 25-30
- 20-25
- 15-20
- 10-15
- 5-10
- 0-5

Language Arts

26. According to the title, what land area is shown?

_____

27. What does the title tell you about the topic of this map?

_____

28. How many symbols are included in the map key?

_____

29. What is the smallest area represented by a symbol from the map key?

_____

30. What state contains this area?

_____

31. Examine the map key and the areas on the map that correspond to these symbols. Does the likelihood of F4 tornadoes increase or decrease as one moves away from the hardest hit area?

_____

32. Which area will never be hit by an F4 tornado according to this map?

_____

_____

33. If the hardest hit area experiences 40 F4 tornadoes in 1,000 years, do you think the odds are good that most people living in the area will experience one of these storms? Why or why not?

_____

_____

_____

_____

Open-Ended
Question

34. Use a separate piece of paper or write in your literary response journal. Refer to the information in this lesson.

- Why might maps need to be changed through the years in order to show the areas where hurricanes, tornadoes, and other storms occur?

- What kinds of factors might change the habitats or migration routes of birds like the bobolink?

Extension Activities

Viewing Prompt ● Examining Weather Maps

Individual Activity

35. Find the weather map in your local or state newspaper. What do the symbols on the map represent? Find these symbols on the weather map. What kind of weather is predicted for your area today? What is the weather supposed to be like in neighboring states? Which of these states is experiencing a weather system that is supposed to move toward your state? How will the change in weather affect people's daily activities? Write a brief report about the weather for today and a prediction for the next few days. Take notes about the weather for the next few days to check how accurate the map was in making weather predictions.

_____

_____

_____

Writing Prompt ● Planning the Ultimate Vacation

Cooperative Group Activity

36. Work with a group. Talk about exotic places around the world that the members would like to visit. Make a list of these locations and find them on a world map. Use an atlas, maps from encyclopedias, or other kinds of maps to locate highways and other routes that can be used to reach these spots. Which spots can be reached by traveling over land? Which ones can only be reached by plane or ship? What do the maps tell you about the sights you might see in traveling to these areas? Plan a route showing how the group could travel so that all the locations are visited in an around-the-world tour. Draw a map showing this route. Add labels to your map, and be sure to describe the types of transportation that would be used, why each one was chosen, and how the act of traveling from one place to another can be as exciting as visiting the exotic places. Share your map with the class.

_____

_____

Speaking Prompt ● Using Critical-Thinking Skills

Workplace Readiness Activity

37. Work with a group. Discuss the kind of career you would like to pursue. What are some of the nation's companies and businesses that employ people in these kinds of jobs? Go on-line and search the Internet or conduct research in the library to identify national and international corporations that might employ students with your interests. Where do these companies have offices? Are these offices located in one state or in many states? Which companies have offices in other countries? What kinds of skills would employees need in order to be considered for a job overseas? Use a map to make a group speech about the companies you have studied.

_____

_____

 Language Arts

Classroom
Discussion

Why do families take photographs? How are these photos different from the ones included in newspapers and magazines? How is a drawing different from a photograph?

Classroom
Activity

Read and examine the information below. Answer the questions that follow.

Pictures and photographs are created to help viewers get an idea of what an event looked like. Photographers are always on hand when something important has been planned, such as the inauguration of a new President of the United States. Artists often commemorate important events by creating paintings or drawings. Before the invention of photography in the early and middle 1800s, only drawings and paintings could be used to depict important occasions. Remember, however, that a drawing or painting shows the artist's idea of an event or occasion. Photographers can also manipulate items in a photo to portray a certain idea or theme. Careful examination of pictures and photographs will help you understand not only what is shown, but the idea that the artist or photographer is trying to convey.

Lesson 2

Step 1

Determine the topic of the photograph.

1. **What kind of geographic area is shown in the photograph?**

_____

Step 2

Examine the details shown in the photograph.

2. **What kinds of natural land features are shown in this photograph?**

_____

3. **Where are the trees growing in this location?**

_____

4. **How have people left their mark on this spot?**

_____

5. **Which area has little vegetation or other signs of life?**

_____

Step 3

Make decisions about the photograph based on the details you identified.

6. **What is the weather like? How can you tell?**

_____

_____

7. **How can you tell that the water is a lake and not a river?**

_____

8. **Is the photographer standing on high or low ground? How can you tell?**

_____

9. **Suppose you are told that the open ground has blocked the water so that it now is a lake instead of a river. What might have caused the land to block the water?**

_____

10. **Why do you think the photographer climbed so high to take this photograph?**

_____

_____

_____

_____

 Language Arts

Lesson 2

Open-Ended Question

11. Think about your answer to the following question. Write your answer on the lines. Be prepared to talk about your answer in a classroom discussion. Why do you think people are so fascinated with scenes showing the results of natural disasters?

_____

_____

_____

_____

_____

_____

_____

Ideas to Remember

> **picture**–a visual presentation that is drawn in order to give facts, ideas, and stories for viewers to examine
>
> **photograph**–a visual presentation that is taken with a camera and printed on paper in order to give facts, ideas, and stories for viewers to examine

Guided Practice Activity

Examine the picture shown below. Answer the questions that follow.

GO TO NEXT PAGE

Step 1

Determine the topic of the picture.

12. **What kind of event is shown in this drawing?**

_____

Step 2

Examine the details shown in the picture.

13. **How many people are shown taking part in this event?**

_____

14. **What is the gender of these people?**

_____

15. **What is special about the ribbon the people are about to reach?**

_____

Step 3

Make decisions about the picture based on the details you identified.

16. **Who will win the race? How can you tell?**

_____

17. **Has this runner had an easy or a tough run? How can you tell?**

_____

_____

18. **What will cause the last runner to come in third?**

_____

19. **What can you tell about the preparations made for the race by the appearances of the three people?**

_____

_____

_____

20. **What do you think the artist is trying to say about the race by varying the runners' appearances?**

_____

_____

_____

Application
Activity

Examine the photograph shown below. Answer the questions that follow.

21. **What is the topic of this photograph?**

_____

22. **How many people are shown?**

_____

23. **What are the people doing?**

_____

24. **What country are these people from? How can you tell?**

_____

25. **What time of day is shown? How can you tell?**

_____

26. **What is forming the shadow that can be seen on the ground?**

_____

27. **What is the atmosphere like in this place? How can you tell?**

_____

_____

28. Do you think this was a good place for a landing? Why or why not?

_____

_____

_____

_____

Open-Ended Question

29. Use a separate piece of paper or write in your literary response journal. Refer to the information in this lesson.

- What kinds of personality traits do you believe it takes to make a good astronaut?

- Should the United States continue its exploration of space and other planets? Why or why not?

Extension Activities

Viewing Prompt ● Reviewing Historical Pictures and Photographs

Individual Activity

30. Look through your history or social studies textbook. What kinds of illustrations are included in this book? What are the topics of some of these pictures and photographs? Choose a chapter that has drawings and photographs that illustrate a particular period in history. How do the pictures differ from the photographs in the ways in which they depict events? How are their purposes alike? Which is the most effective illustration in the chapter? What makes it so interesting? Share your ideas by giving a short speech to the class.

_____

_____

_____

_____

_____

_____

_____

_____

_____

Language Arts

Speaking Prompt ● Analyzing Illustrations

**Cooperative
Group
Activity**

31. **Work with a group. Find photographs and pictures from old magazines and newspapers. Cut out these illustrations, make notes about the captions and other labels included with the illustrations, and present them to the group. Do not let the group know what the captions and text tell about the pictures and photographs. Talk about each illustration, its details, and what you can tell about the scene from these details. Compare the group's ideas to the information included in the captions and text. How accurate were the group's analyses of each picture and photograph?**

_____

_____

_____

_____

_____

_____

_____

Writing Prompt ● Analyzing Technology

**Workplace
Readiness
Activity**

32. **Work with a group. Research the use of cameras in the workplace today. What kinds of businesses rely on cameras to carry out business? How do photographs enable these companies to function? How has technology changed the kinds of cameras that are used by businesses? Why have computers become an important tool in photography? Which of these careers might be of interest to the members of the group? What special skills and technical knowledge will the members need to have in order to be considered for these kinds of jobs? How strong will the demand be in the future for people who want to work in these fields? Prepare a group report describing the results of your research.**

_____

_____

_____

_____

_____

_____

_____

_____

Classroom
Discussion

How can information be organized so that it is easy to see similarities and differences among the types of information? What kinds of information are best organized by which kinds of graphics?

Classroom
Activity

Read and examine the information below. Answer the questions that follow.

A special illustration that organizes information is a graphic. There are different kinds of graphics, and each is best suited for different kinds of information. **Tables** are best at organizing simple lists of information. **Charts** use columns and rows so that viewers can compare the sets of information in the charts. **Circle graphs** show how different parts make up one complete idea or concept. **Bar graphs** allow viewers to see the differences among various categories or ideas. **Line graphs** are used to show how quantities change over time.

Figure A: Table

| Deaths Caused by Hurricanes ||
Year	Deaths
1900	6,000 people in Galveston, Texas
1928	1,800 people in Lake Okeechobee, Florida, and 300 people in Puerto Rico
1963	5,000 people in Haiti; 1,700 people in Cuba; and 400 people in the Dominican Republic
1974	8,000 people in Honduras
1976	400 people in Baja California Sur, Mexico

Figure B: Chart

The Fujita Scale		
Type of Tornado	**Wind Speed**	**Type of Damage**
F0	40–72 mph	Chimneys are damaged, and branches are broken out of trees.
F1	73–112 mph	Mobile homes are blown over.
F2	113–157 mph	Trees are pulled out of the ground, and mobile homes are destroyed.
F3	158–205 mph	Roofs and walls of buildings collapse, and trains and cars are blown over.
F4	205–260 mph	Strong walls of buildings collapse.
F5	261–318 mph	Homes and buildings are destroyed.

mph = miles per hour

Step 1

Determine the topic of the graphic.

1. **Look at the title of Figure A. What is the topic of this table?**

   _____

2. **Look at title of Figure B. What is the topic of this chart?**

   _____

Decide how information is organized in the graphic.

3. What does the first column represent in each graphic?

_____

_____

4. What do the numbers in each graphic represent?

_____

_____

_____

5. What kinds of facts are compared in the chart?

_____

_____

6. What kinds of facts are compared in the table?

_____

7. Which graphic–a table or a chart–allows a viewer to compare more than one fact about a topic?

_____

Make decisions about the topics by analyzing the details included in the graphics.

8. What areas of North America have been hit by hurricanes?

_____

9. How have the hurricanes been different through the years?

_____

_____

10. What characteristic of a tornado is measured to determine its place on the Fujita scale?

_____

11. Does damage increase or decrease in relation to the speed of the wind in tornadoes?

_____

Open-Ended
Question

12. Think about your answer to the following question. Write your answer on the lines. Be prepared to talk about your answer in a classroom discussion. How do the lives of people change after they survive direct hits from hurricanes and tornadoes?

_____

_____

_____

_____

_____

_____

_____

_____

_____

Ideas to
Remember

> **table**–a graphic that compares simple columns of data
>
> **circle graph**–a graphic that shows how parts compare to the whole
>
> **chart**–a graphic that uses columns and rows to present and compare information
>
> **line graph**–a graphic that uses line segments on a grid to show how amounts or values change over time
>
> **bar graph**–a graphic that uses vertical or horizontal bars on a grid to compare numbers or amounts

Guided
Practice
Activity

Examine the graphs shown below. Then answer the questions that follow.

Figure C: Circle Graph

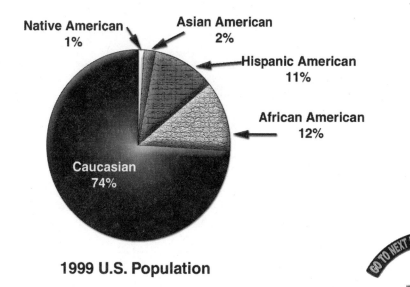

1999 U.S. Population

Figure D: Bar Graph

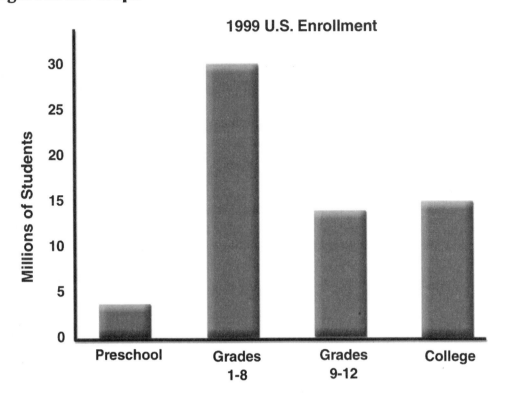

1999 U.S. Enrollment

Figure E: Line Graph

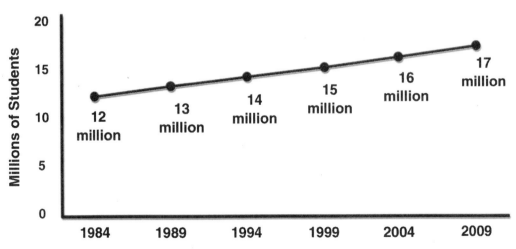

U.S. College Enrollment

 Language Arts

GO TO NEXT PAGE

Step 1

Determine the topic of the graphic.

13. Look at the titles of the figures. What is the topic of each graphic?

_____

_____

Step 2

Decide how information is organized in the graphic.

14. Which kinds of graphics show quantities?

_____

15. Which graphs show quantities for only one year?

_____

16. Which graph shows quantities for more than one year?

_____

17. Which graph can be used to determine how enrollment has changed through the years?

_____

18. Which graph can be used to see how different parts make up one complete idea or basic set of information?

_____

19. How is size used to compare quantities in the bar and circle graphs?

_____

_____

20. How is the difference in quantity shown on a line graph?

_____

Step 3

Make decisions about the topics by analyzing the details included in the graphics.

21. Did college enrollment increase or decrease from 1984 to 1999?

_____

22. How is college enrollment expected to change after the year 2000?

_____

23. What was the largest group of students enrolled in the United States in 1999?

_____

24. If enrollment was divided in half between Grades 1–4 and Grades 5–8, about how many students would be in each group?

_____

25. Would this new division be about the same, less than, or greater than enrollment in college?

_____

26. What group makes up the largest percentage of the U.S. population?

_____

27. How does the percentage of African Americans compare to the percentages for Hispanic Americans, Asian Americans, and Native Americans?

_____

_____

_____

Application Activity

Read each paragraph below. Use the information in the paragraphs to complete the graphs. Then answer the questions that follow.

28. Students who own home computers find them useful for different kinds of things. Of these students, 88 percent write special reports on their home computers. Eighty-five percent use home computers to conduct research with CD roms and on the Internet. Special educational software is run by 54 percent of these students. Half, or 50 percent, use their computers to complete their homework. Chatting with friends is a pastime for 43 percent of the students who own home computers.

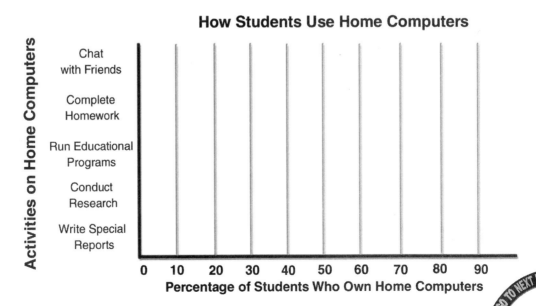

29. High school enrollment has changed through the years. In 1984 there were 13 million high school students in the United States. This number had dropped to 10 million in 1989, but increased to 12 million in 1994. Growth by another 2 million made U.S. enrollment in high schools reach 14 million in 1999. The federal government expects there to be 16 million high school students in 2004, and 18 million in 2009.

U.S. High School Enrollment (Grades 9-12)

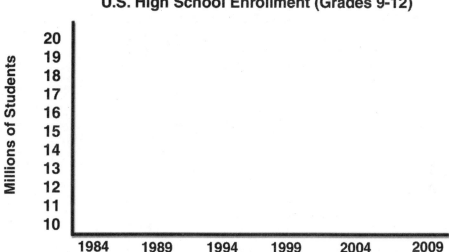

30. What will be the makeup of U.S. schools in 2009? About 26% of the students will be enrolled in Grades 9 - 12. About 24% will be college students. Only 7% of students will be enrolled in preschool, while Grades 1 - 8 will make up 43% of the students who are enrolled in U.S. schools.

**U.S. Enrollment in 2009
(Preschool through College)**

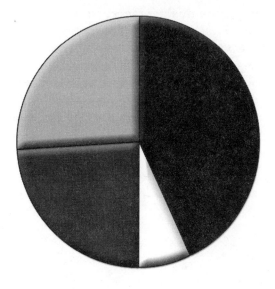

31. Why do you think so many students use home computers to prepare special reports?

_____

_____

_____

32. How long did it take for high school enrollment to exceed the numbers for 1984?

_____

33. According to the graph, do most high-school seniors seem to go on to college? How can you tell?

_____

_____

_____

Open-Ended Question

34. Use a separate piece of paper or write in your literary response journal. Refer to the information in this lesson.

- Do you believe that a computer is an essential tool for students to use in today's schools? Why or why not?

- Why should students be careful in selecting sites on the Internet when conducting research on the worldwide web?

Extension Activities

Writing Prompt ● Graphing Weather Patterns

Individual Activity

35. Watch the weather report on television each evening, or examine the weather section of your local newspaper. Take notes about the high temperature and low temperature predicted each day for a week. Plot these predictions on a line graph. Note the actual high and low temperature for each day, and plot these facts on a second line graph. How accurately did the weather reporters predict what the temperatures would be? On which days were their predictions closest to the actual temperatures? What special weather occurrences might have affected the temperatures for each day? Share your findings with the class.

_____

_____

_____

_____

_____

Language Arts

Lesson 3

Writing Prompt ● Graphing Various Statistics

Cooperative Group Activity

36. **Work with a group. Talk about the ways in which members of the group are alike and different. For example, you might discuss age, hair color, height, family size, career goals, and other characteristics. Which sets of facts can be displayed on line graphs? Which can be displayed on bar graphs and on circle graphs? Create a line graph, a bar graph, and a circle graph by using some of the facts you discuss. Place these graphs on a poster and include a paragraph with each graph that explains the conclusions that can be drawn about the people who made up the group. Display your poster in the classroom.**

_____

_____

_____

_____

_____

_____

_____

_____

_____

Speaking Prompt ● Using Critical-Thinking Skills

Workplace Readiness Activity

37. **Work with a group. List the kinds of careers that the members are considering for the future. Go online, conduct research in the library, or talk with your school's guidance counselor to find out about these careers. How has demand for people with these skills changed over the years? How have salaries changed since the 1980s? How many people now enrolled in college are preparing for jobs in these areas? What will be the demand for each kind of job in the future? Compile your research by organizing the results on graphs. Present your graphs to the class and lead a discussion about the information they present.**

_____

_____

_____

_____

_____

_____

_____

_____

_____

_____

Analyzing Visual Presentations

Taking Notes from Films and Videos

Classroom
Discussion

How are movies like novels or plays? How are they different? Are some stories better suited to being made into a film than others? What story would you like to see made into a film?

Classroom
Activity

Read and examine the information below. Then answer the questions that follow.

As you take notes on a novel or short story, you look for the topic, the central idea, and details about the opening, setting, characters, and plot. The same method can be used when you watch a movie. Movies share many of the elements of a novel or a play. Besides the details of the story, you can analyze such features as the music, lighting, camera work, costumes, special effects, and acting performances.

Read this review of Woody Allen's 1985 film *The Purple Rose of Cairo*. Notice all the elements of film-making that the reviewer mentions.

Have you ever wished that the glamorous star of a Hollywood movie could step off the screen and join you in real life? That's the idea behind director Woody Allen's marvelous comedy *The Purple Rose of Cairo*. Cecilia (Mia Farrow) is a forlorn waitress whose one pleasure in life is going to the movies. Her favorite star is Gil Shepherd (Jeff Daniels), or rather the adventurous character Gil plays, "Tom Baxter." One afternoon, while Cecilia is watching the movie-within-a-movie (which is also called *The Purple Rose of Cairo*) for the fifth time, Tom Baxter suddenly notices her from the screen. Pleased that she likes the movie so well, he steps off the screen to speak to her. In an instant, black-and-white Tom becomes full-color flesh-and-blood Tom, to the alarm of the other characters on the screen and the members of the audience. Only Cecilia is delighted by this odd event—her dreams have become a reality.

But Tom's entrance into the real world has hilarious consequences. With Tom gone, the other characters in the black-and-white film are at a loss. They can't go on with the story and they argue over what to do next. Soon the actor Gil Shepherd arrives from Hollywood in hopes of talking his character, Tom Baxter, back onto the screen. Eventually he succeeds, but not before Cecilia, Tom, and the other characters go through some incredible complications. By the end, Cecilia has learned a painful lesson about the difference between fantasy and reality.

Every detail in the film plays up the contrast between the glamorous world on the movie screen and the rather drab surroundings of Cecilia's everyday life. The colors of the "real" scenes look rather washed-out, while the black-and-white movie scenes appear silvery and glamorous, like the Hollywood films of the 1930s. Most of the characters, including Cecilia, wear the simple clothes of the Depression era. This sets up a perfect contrast with the dashing Tom Baxter, in his pith helmet and explorer's duds. As usual, Woody Allen uses old jazz music from the 1930s to set up a mood of wistful romance. As Cecilia, Mia Farrow gives a fine performance, emphasizing the character's sweetness and her quiet longing for romance. Jeff Daniels' Tom Baxter is a great creation: he has a hero's confidence about things that he's done in the plots of his movies, but ordinary skills, like starting a real-life automobile, escape him. Tom, like most of the things Cecilia loves about the movies, is just too good to be true.

GO TO NEXT PAGE

 Language Arts

Step 1

Identify the topic of the film.

1. **What is the topic, or subject, of *The Purple Rose of Cairo*?**

_____

_____

_____

Step 2

Identify the central idea of the film.

2. **What is the central idea of *The Purple Rose of Cairo*?**

_____

_____

Step 3

Identify details about the plot.

3. **Why did the character "Tom Baxter" step off the screen to join Cecilia?**

_____

4. **How do the other characters in the black-and-white film react when Tom steps off the screen?**

_____

_____

5. **How does Cecilia react when Tom steps off the screen?**

_____

6. **What happens to make Tom return to the screen?**

_____

_____

Step 4

Identify details about how the film was made.

7. **Who is the director of *The Purple Rose of Cairo*?**

_____

8. **How does the director use color to emphasize the difference between fantasy and reality?**

_____

_____

9. How do the costumes show the difference between fantasy and reality?

_____

_____

10. What mood does the film's music create?

_____

11. What does the reviewer think of Mia Farrow's performance?

_____

_____

Open-Ended Question

12. Think about your answer to the following question. Write your answer on the lines. Be prepared to talk about your answer in a classroom discussion. What character from a movie would you like to meet in real life and why?

_____

_____

_____

_____

_____

_____

_____

_____

_____

_____

Ideas to Remember

film–a filmed story with a plot, characters, setting, and costumes

film-making–the elements that go into making a film, such as lighting, setting, costumes, camera work, etc.

director–the person who controls the artistic elements in a film

special effects–effects used to create an illusion in a film, such as a bomb exploding

Language Arts

Guided
Practice
Activity

Read the movie review below. Look for details about the elements of film-making. Then answer the questions that follow.

In 1941 Orson Welles directed his first motion picture, *Citizen Kane*. Based loosely on the life of newspaper tycoon William Randolph Hearst, the picture was a breakthrough in all sorts of ways. Welles, who'd begun his show business career on radio, used the movie studio like a pianist manipulates the keyboard. With imagination and a great sense of humor, Welles showed just how entertaining a serious movie could be.

Citizen Kane tells the story of Charles Foster Kane, a lonely, aging millionaire who has pushed away everyone who ever loved him in his long life. The film reveals Kane's life in a series of flashbacks and "interviews" with Kane's former wives, friends, and employees. Kane is shown to be a talented but selfish person whose money can buy everything but love and friendship. At the end his dying word "Rosebud" is found to be a connection to his childhood—the last time when he'd felt loved and wanted.

Welles uses every camera trick he can think of to tell his story. One camera technique was called deep focus, which allowed every detail in a shot to remain in focus from front to back. This method led to wonderful optical illusions in the film, such as the scene of Kane signing away his newspaper before a normal-sized set of windows; as he drifts toward the back of the office, we realize the windows are actually huge, making Kane look as small as he feels at that moment. Welles also used real ceilings in the studio. This allowed him to shoot upwards, showing his characters from below. He employed a variety of tracking shots, in which the camera moves up or down or slides along to follow the action. In one famous shot, when Kane's young wife is having her debut as an opera singer, the camera rises and rises above the stage until it finds a pair of stagehands in the wings, one holding his nose in response to the singing.

The lighting in the movie is filled with contrasts. Kane's mansion is dark and gloomy, to show the loneliness of his old age. Huge shadows precede characters across walls and down staircases. The sunny interiors of Kane's early life leads to the darkness and emptiness of his end. At one point the older Kane walks in front of some mirrors and his image multiplies into dozens of Kanes receding into the distance.

With his experience in radio, Welles played with the sound of the film as well. The dialogue in *Citizen Kane* overlaps, as people interrupt each other or talk all at once, just as they do in real life. All sorts of voices are heard, from Kane's booming speech at a political rally to the sobs and screeches of his young wife living a lonely life in their huge mansion.

The acting in *Kane* is also extraordinary. Welles is perfect as the self-centered tycoon whose endless charm can't make up for his inability to connect with other people. Joseph Cotten plays a former friend of Kane's who sees right through all his plots and schemes. As Kane's young wife, Dorothy Comingore gives a touching performance. She easily expresses the pain and confusion of a simple girl whose life is turned upside down by Kane and his millions.

At its release, *Citizen Kane* was not a hit. The public didn't quite know what to make of such a strange uncompromising picture. But now the public and critics alike agree that *Kane* is one of the greatest motion pictures ever made.

Step 1

Identify the topic of the film.

13. What is the topic, or subject, of *Citizen Kane*?

_____

_____

Step 2

Identify the central idea of the film.

14. What is the central idea of *Citizen Kane*?

_____

_____

Step 3

Identify details about how the film was made.

15. What is deep focus and how was it used in *Citizen Kane*?

_____

_____

_____

16. Why did Welles have real ceilings built for his sets?

_____

17. What is a tracking shot?

_____

18. What is special about the lighting effects in *Citizen Kane*?

_____

_____

19. What is special about the dialogue in *Citizen Kane*?

_____

_____

20. What is special about Dorothy Comingore's performance as Kane's young wife?

_____

_____

Language Arts

Lesson 4

Step 4

Record your own opinions about the film or the review.

21. Does this review make you want to see *Citizen Kane*? Explain your answer.

_____

22. What parts of the film should the reviewer have described in more detail?

_____

_____

Application Activity

Choose a movie that you've **never seen before**. Watch it in the media center at school, on a VCR at home, or on network television. As you watch, take notes on the kinds of information featured in this lesson. Use your notes to answer the following questions.

23. What was the topic of this film?

_____

_____

_____

24. What was the central idea or theme of this film?

_____

_____

_____

25. What are the main details of the plot? List them in order.

_____

_____

_____

26. What is the setting for this film?

_____

_____

_____

27. Who are the main characters?

_____

_____

_____

28. How does the film's ending resolve all the plot elements?

_____

_____

_____

_____

29. What elements of film-making can you comment on in this movie?

_____

_____

_____

_____

30. How well do the actors portray their characters? Who stands out and why?

_____

_____

_____

_____

31. What was your overall impression of this film?

_____

_____

_____

_____

Open-Ended Question

32. Use a separate piece of paper or write in your literary response journal. Refer to the information in this lesson.

Some film directors, like Woody Allen, Jane Campion, and Spike Lee, like to control every detail of their movie productions.

● If you could write and direct your own film, what would be its topic and central theme?

● What elements of film-making would you concentrate on in your movie?

Extension Activities

Viewing Prompt ● Creating a Storyboard of a Movie Scene

Individual Activity

33. A storyboard is like a comic strip version of a movie scene. Each panel shows a camera shot, including the setting and the characters' actions. For example, a storyboard might show a scene of a girl hitting a home run in softball. The first panel would feature her swing. The next panel would show the reaction of the crowd. The third panel would show the arc of the ball heading towards the fence, and so forth. Choose a scene from a movie on video and watch it several times. Then create a storyboard of the scene. Don't worry about your drawing style; rough sketches will work fine. Label the panels of your storyboard to describe the important elements of each camera shot.

_____

_____

_____

Writing Prompt ● Writing a Movie Review

Cooperative Group Activity

34. Work with a partner. Watch a recent movie on video at home or in the media center at school. As you watch, take notes on the major elements of the film and how it was made. Use your notes to write a review of the movie. In your review, include both factual descriptions of what is in the film and your opinions about the film. Get together with your partner and take turns reading your reviews aloud. Discuss the different elements of the film and how they affected the overall quality of the film. Be prepared to defend your opinions about the movie using details from the plot, the characters, and the production values. Make suggestions to improve each other's review. Then see if you can publish your review on the Internet or post it on a bulletin board for other movie fans to read.

_____

_____

_____

Speaking Prompt ● Describe the Importance of Academic and Occupational Skills

Workplace Readiness Activity

35. Work with a group. Hold a discussion about the various kinds of jobs available in the movie industry or in making independent films. Emphasize that the high-profile jobs of directing and acting form only a small part of the many jobs available. For example, a person with a talent for sculpting or painting might work in the special effects department creating masks, fake creatures, or miniature landscapes. Make notes on the different kinds of jobs in film-making. Divide into smaller groups and choose one of the jobs to research. Find out what academic skills are needed to perform that job as well as any special skills or training. When you gather with the large group again, take turns making reports on the information you found. If possible, invite someone who has worked in the film industry to speak to the group. Later, discuss which job in the film industry appeals to you most and why.

_____

_____

Classroom Discussion

What things might be different about a story if it is written in book form or presented as a play? What movies or plays have you seen that are based on a book or another kind of source?

Classroom Activity

Often stories, characters, or ideas that appear in one media source have been adapted from another kind of source. For instance, have you seen any movies that featured a Frankenstein monster? Did you know that the original version was a novel by Mary Shelley called *Frankenstein*, which is considered a classic in literature?

Another example is *Little Orphan Annie*. It began as a popular cartoon strip decades ago. Annie had no parents and no real home, and she lived alone with her dog Sandy. Annie had frizzy red hair, and her eyes were round ovals with no pupils or irises. She wore a red dress with a white collar, a white belt, and white cuffs. Sandy was a big red dog whose only sound was "Arf." Annie and Sandy solved mysteries and helped bring criminals to justice. They were often in danger, including Annie being kidnapped and held hostage. Even though Sandy and Annie must have lived on the streets, Annie's dress rarely got dirty, and if it did, it was magically clean and pressed by the next episode. If Annie got into too much danger, Punjab, a middle-eastern man who wore a turban, showed up to help her. He was the valet of Annie's protector, Daddy Warbucks. Sandy also helped to get Annie out of trouble if he could. Even though Daddy Warbucks protected Annie and took care of her in dangerous situations, he never gave Annie a home or fed her. Annie was pretty much on her own unless she was in serious trouble.

In 1977 a Broadway musical named *Annie* was created, based on the story of *Little Orphan Annie*. The star is a little red-haired girl with tousled curls. She has a dog named Sandy, and she lives in the Hudson Street Home for Girls. In the musical and in the film by the same name, released in 1982, Daddy Warbucks is a wealthy but harsh man who wants to improve his public image. He decides to take an orphan into his home for one week. Annie, who has tried repeatedly to run away from the orphanage, manages to get the invitation to visit Warbucks. He is so taken with her that, after a week, he decides to adopt her permanently. However, Annie declines, saying that her real parents possess the other half of a pendant she wears around her neck, and that they will return for her someday. It is then revealed to the audience that Annie's parents died in a fire, and all their remaining possessions are at the orphanage, including the missing half of Annie's pendant. When Warbucks offers $50,000 for the return of Annie's parents, Miss Hannigan, the head of the orphanage, gets her accomplices, Rooster and Lily, to act as Annie's parents and take the money. She gives them the missing half of Annie's pendant, and they go to claim Annie and the fortune. Warbucks finds out about the deception, tracks them down, and finally adopts Annie.

In the Broadway and movie versions, *Annie* does not solve crimes and fight criminals. She is never in grave danger, and Sandy and Punjab never have to save her life. She does not live on the streets, but in an institution. At best, the Broadway musical and film *Annie* are loosely based on the cartoon *Little Orphan Annie*.

GO TO NEXT PAGE

Step 1

Identify what kind of work is being adapted.

1. In what entertainment medium did the original *Little Orphan Annie* appear?

_____

2. How is this entertainment medium created?

_____

3. Where did the original Annie live and what did she do?

_____

_____

Step 2

Identify what medium the work is adapted into.

4. What entertainment medium was *Little Orphan Annie* adapted into in 1977? Circle the letter of your answer.

a. film   c. radio

b. television   d. musical

5. What entertainment medium was *Little Orphan Annie* adapted into in 1982? Circle the letter of your answer.

a. film   c. radio

b. television   d. musical

Step 3

Identify how the original was adapted to make a new work.

6. What degree of danger was the original Annie in?

_____

_____

7. Where did the original Annie and Sandy live?

_____

8. What degree of danger is the film Annie in?

_____

9. Is her life really in danger?

_____

10. Where does the film Annie live?

_____

11. What is the difference in the original Daddy Warbucks and the film character?

_____

_____

Open-Ended Question

12. Think about your answer to the following question. Write your answer on the lines. Be prepared to talk about your answer in a classroom discussion. Knowing that the *Little Orphan Annie* comic strip was created in the 1930s, why do you think people accepted the fact that Annie and her dog lived alone on the streets and were in life-threatening danger so much?

_____

_____

_____

_____

_____

_____

_____

_____

Ideas to Remember

> **adapt**—to use stories, characters, or ideas from one media source to create a work in another medium

Guided Practice Activity

Read the following paragraphs. Then follow the steps and answer the questions.

Edgar Allen Poe's short story "The Fall of the House of Usher" is an example of how one's own terrors can be more horrible than anyone else can inflict. In this story, Roderick Usher sends for an old school friend to visit at his country home. When the friend arrives, he first notices that the house is sitting in the middle of a marsh, and its walls are cracked and crumbling. The stranger continues across a short bridge and into the home, where he is encountered by his school friend Roderick, who has grown pale and thin and is in an excited and nervous state. Roderick confides to the friend that all his senses are heightened lately—sounds are too loud and hurt his ears; the taste of food is too strong; his clothes feel rough and scratchy; and the slightest bit of light hurts his eyes. While the two of them talk, a ghostly figure passes through the room and goes up the stairs. Roderick tells the friend that the figure is his sister Madeline, who has been ill, but doctors cannot find the cause of her illness.

Later that night Madeline dies. The doctor is summoned, and Roderick asks his friend to help him bury Madeline. The next night, the two men carry her coffin down into the basement of the house. The lower room is covered in copper, and an iron gate closes off half the room from the other section. When the two open the coffin to look at Madeline one last time, Roderick tells his friend that he and Madeline are twins. The narrator confesses that Madeline does not look as if she is dead. Her lips have a faint smile on them and her cheeks seem to blush. Roderick says that Madeline's appearance is symptomatic of her illness.

GO TO NEXT PAGE

Two weeks later, the two men are in the drawing room. Roderick is pacing the floor in a frenzy while his friend reads aloud to try and calm him. At various times during the reading, noises can be heard outside the door, and with each sound, Roderick becomes more agitated. A loud scraping and tearing noise can be heard along with a pounding sound. Finally, Roderick screams that Madeline is still alive and is standing outside the door. The wind blows the door open, and Madeline staggers into the room, covered with blood from clawing her way out of the coffin. She dies and falls onto Roderick, who dies of fright.

The friend and narrator of the story prepares to leave the house. As he rides over the bridge he crossed on his arrival, he hears a low rumble. He turns to see the house crumble and fall into the marsh.

Poe's story was turned into a movie entitled *House of Usher*, starring Vincent Price as Roderick Usher. The film opens as Philip Winthrop approaches the Usher home, which is built in a scorched and burned landscape. Winthrop is engaged to Madeline Usher, and he meets Roderick for the first time. Madeline seems pale and ill, and her brother Roderick is bothered by heightened senses. On his visit, Philip learns that the Usher family has been involved in crime, many of the members have been insane, and now Madeline and Roderick, the last of the family have been broken under the weight of the horrors of the family. Both the house and the land around it seem consumed with evil.

Roderick resents the presence of Philip because he loves his sister and does not want her to marry, and so he forbids it. Philip plans to sneak Madeline out of the house, but she dies suddenly. After she is sealed in the family tomb under the house, Roderick confides to Philip that Madeline was a victim of sudden death-like trances. Philip has nightmares of Madeline screaming in her coffin. Finally Roderick admits that he has buried his sister alive and he can hear her trying to get out of her coffin. Philip runs to open the coffin, but he is too late. Madeline, bloody from her struggles and insane from being buried prematurely, has gotten out. She leaps at her brother, and both of them struggle and die. The house bursts into flames.

Philip flees the burning house and turns to see it sink into the ground.

While Poe does not establish a relationship between the friend and Madeline, the film indicates that the two were to be married. The visitor, in Poe's story, is a friend of Roderick, while in the film, the visitor meets Roderick for the first time. In the film, Roderick is Madeline's older brother, while Poe creates a special bond by making them twins. In the short story, Roderick fears that Madeline may have still been alive when they buried her, but in the film, Roderick buries Madeline alive on purpose—to keep her from marrying Philip. In both the film and the story, Madeline claws her way out of the coffin and dies. In the story, she falls onto Roderick and he dies of fright. In the film, she leaps at Roderick in an attempt to injure him for burying her. The writers of the film stay fairly close to the original, but they create an engagement between Philip and Madeline that, perhaps, makes the story more believable and provides more than one catalyst to move the action forward.

Lesson 5

Compare and Contrast Media Sources

Step 1

Identify what kind of work is being adapted.

13. In what entertainment medium did the original *"Fall of the House of Usher"* appear?

_____

14. In what form was the original?

_____

Step 2

Identify what medium the work is adapted into.

15. What entertainment medium was "The Fall of the House of Usher" adapted into? Circle the letter of your answer.

a. film   c. radio

b. play   d. television

Step 3

Identify how the original was adapted to make a new work.

16. How is the relationship between Philip and Madeline different from the story to the film?

_____

_____

17. What causes Madeline to be buried alive in the story and the film?

_____

_____

18. What is the main difference between the story by Poe and the film, and how does it affect the plot of the film?

_____

_____

_____

                    Language Arts

Application Activity

Read the information below. Then answer the questions that follow.

Shakespeare's *Romeo and Juliet* is a love story that has been presented in many forms. Franco Zefferelli even made a movie about the couple that is considered one of the greatest love stories ever filmed. It is named *Romeo and Juliet* and stars Leonard Whiting and Olivia Hussey. It is Shakespeare's play on film, and almost no changes were made. Another film, however, has been done that might be called a modern-day *Romeo and Juliet*. This film is entitled *West Side Story*. It was first a musical on Broadway, with a score by Leonard Bernstein, and then a film.

In *Romeo and Juliet*, two families—the Capulets and Montagues—are involved in a feud that has been going on for years. No member of either house can tolerate the presence of any member of the other house. Then, fatefully, Romeo and Juliet meet at a dance and fall in love. Knowing that their families will not approve, they see each other in secret. Juliet's nurse helps her hide the fact that she is seeing Romeo. Eventually the two marry in secret. They have very little time together before Mercutio, a friend of Romeo, is killed by Juliet's cousin Tybalt, who in turn is slain by Romeo. On the advice of the priest who married them, Romeo leaves the city. Meanwhile, Juliet devises a plan by which she will take a sleeping potion that will make her seem dead. After her family has put her into the tomb, Romeo will come to see her, she will awake and tell him the truth, and the two will run off together. The priest sends a messenger to tell Romeo of her plan, but he is stopped on his mission, and Romeo never learns of the plot. When he hears that Juliet is dead, he goes to her tomb to mourn. He has brought a vial of poison with him. In Juliet's tomb, Romeo drinks the poison and dies. Juliet awakes to find him dead, and she is so grief-stricken that she kills herself with Romeo's dagger.

In *West Side Story*, two street gangs—the Sharks and the Jets—are involved in a feud. A former Jets gang member, Tony, has met Maria, a sister of one of the Sharks, and fallen in love with her. The two gangs spar with each other from time to time. All the while, Maria and Tony see each other in secret and plan how to run away so that they can marry. The two rival gangs plan a rumble, and everyone prepares for trouble. Tony decides that he will have to appear and stop the fight before someone gets hurt. All the gang members meet in an alley, and the fight begins. While trying to stop the fight, Tony is shot and killed. Maria is left alone to mourn her beloved Tony, while the gang hatred continues.

19. How are *West Side Story* and *Romeo and Juliet* alike? Circle the letter of your answer.

    a. One story is a play and the other is a movie.

    b. The main characters are foolish for getting involved with someone their families wouldn't like.

    c. Both stories are based on families or gangs that are feuding with each other.

20. What is the central theme of both works? Circle the letter of your answer.

    a. Hatred can cause tremendous losses, and can have little gain.

    b. If families have to fight, they should fight to the death.

    c. If you love someone enough, all your troubles will be over.

21. Explain how *West Side Story* can be called an adaptation of *Romeo and Juliet*.

_____

_____

_____

Open-Ended Question

22. Use a separate piece of paper or write in your literary response journal. Refer to the information in the Application Activity.

- With which work—*Romeo and Juliet* or *West Side Story*—do you more closely identify and why?

- Why do you think that producers, writers, and directors adapt and use stories and plays that were written by other people long ago?

Extension Activities

Viewing Prompt ● Comparing Media

Individual Activity

23. Which comic book hero has been the hero of an animated or live-action movie? What are the characteristics of this hero? How was the comic book version of this hero similar to the character shown in the cartoon or the movie? Did these changes improve the character so that he or she was more interesting? Which other comic book stories do you think would make a good cartoon or movie? Why? Write a short report comparing the comic book character with the cartoon or movie version of this character. Share your report with the class.

_____

_____

_____

_____

_____

_____

_____

_____

_____

_____

_____

_____

_____

_____

Language Arts

Speaking Prompt ● Creating a Movie Character

Cooperative Group Activity

24. Work with a small group. Who are some of the people in your school that you admire the most? What are these people like? Which ones make people laugh? Who are the people who are never too busy to help others? Which person do you think will become famous some day? List the character traits of these people. Why would these traits help make colorful characters for a movie? What kinds of adventures would be fun to watch these characters participate in? Create an adventure and a character. Discuss the character and a story line for the person you have created. How will the movie open? What situation will cause problems for the character? How will the character prevail and solve the problem? Members of the group should take turns presenting the character and story line to the class.

_____

_____

_____

_____

_____

_____

_____

Speaking Prompt ● Identify Transferable Occupational Skills

Workplace Readiness Activity

25. Work with a group. Discuss the work of a film reviewer or theater reviewer. What kinds of academic skills would you need to do this job? Would it help to be familiar with a wide range of literature, drama, poetry, and film? What other skills would be valuable for this job? What would be your goal as a reviewer for a magazine or newspaper? Would you target your reviews for a general audience or a more sophisticated viewer? Work together with the group to create a list of the skills needed to be a knowledgeable reviewer. Discuss the list with the rest of the class. Hold a discussion about reviews and how they affect a viewer's decision to see a play or film. Do you generally agree with the reviews you read in the newspaper? Why or why not?

_____

_____

_____

_____

_____

_____

_____

_____

Multiple Choice
Read the following questions and the four possible answers. Choose the answer to each question. Find the bubble next to the question that has the same letter as the answer you chose. Fill in this bubble to mark your answer.

Ⓐ Ⓑ Ⓒ Ⓓ **1. What does a map legend provide?**
  a. details about one particular place   c. a complete list of cities in the world
  b. a main idea about the entire world   d. a list of map symbols and what they represent

Ⓐ Ⓑ Ⓒ Ⓓ **2. Which of the following can be shown on a map?**
  a. the habitat of a certain animal
  b. the area where tornadoes are most likely to occur
  c. the locations of the largest cities in the U.S.
  d. all of the above

Ⓐ Ⓑ Ⓒ Ⓓ **3. Which of the following is used most often nowadays to commemorate an important event?**
  a. drawing   c. etching
  b. photograph   d. painting

Ⓐ Ⓑ Ⓒ Ⓓ **4. Which of the following can be used to convey a particular idea about some person or event?**
  a. drawing   c. painting
  b. photograph   d. all of the above

Ⓐ Ⓑ Ⓒ Ⓓ **5. What kind of graphic is used to organize simple lists of information?**
  a. table   c. bar graph
  b. circle graph   d. line graph

Ⓐ Ⓑ Ⓒ Ⓓ **6. Which kind of graphic shows how parts compare to a whole?**
  a. table   c. bar graph
  b. circle graph   d. line graph

Ⓐ Ⓑ Ⓒ Ⓓ **7. Which is NOT an element of film-making?**
  a. lighting   c. camera work
  b. rhyming   d. acting performances

Ⓐ Ⓑ Ⓒ Ⓓ **8. What do you call the person who controls the artistic elements in a film?**
  a. writer   c. director
  b. producer   d. author

Ⓐ Ⓑ Ⓒ Ⓓ **9. What does "adapt" mean?**
  a. to change from the original literary work   c. to copy an existing work word for word
  b. to create an original work   d. to rename an original work

Ⓐ Ⓑ Ⓒ Ⓓ **10. The stage play *Annie* was adapted from what kind of work?**
  a. novel   c. comic strip
  b. film   d. radio play

Writing Prompt ● You've Seen the Movie, Now Enjoy the TV Show!

Situation

As a television scriptwriter, you've been hired to adapt a popular movie into a weekly 30-minute show on TV. Choose a recent film and write a memo describing the changes you would make to adapt the film into a television show.

Before You Write

As you prepare to write your paper, think about the following ideas:

- How is a feature film different from a television series?

- What other versions of this story exist, such as a novel, play, or comic strip?

- What notes can you make about the most important elements of the movie—such as the topic, central idea, plot, characters, setting, etc.?

- Which of these elements should be changed to make the movie into a TV show?

- How do you want your audience to react to the show?

Write a paper using the situation above as a starting point. Discuss as many elements of the show as possible, and explain why you think certain things should be changed from the movie version. As you write, be sure to think about your topic, main idea or theme, supporting details, opinions, and conclusions. Complete your work on a separate piece of paper. You may wish to write in your literary response journal instead.

Speaking Prompt ● The Place You'd Most Like to Visit

Situation

You've agreed to deliver a speech to the Travel Club about the one place in the world you'd most like to visit. In the speech you'll describe the place and provide details about its attractions.

Before You Speak

As you prepare your speech, think about the following ideas:

- What kind of map can you display to show the location of this place?

- What paintings or photographs could be used to demonstrate the beauty of the place, either in its landscape or in the skyline of its buildings?

- What tables, charts, or graphs could you display to show important facts about this place?

- Is there a movie or documentary on video that you could play for your audience to introduce them to this place?

- What questions might your audience have about this place?

Do research to prepare notes for a speech on the topic above. Deliver the speech to a group of students from your class. Be sure to include a topic, main idea or theme, supporting details, opinions, and conclusions. You can use such things as pictures, photographs, charts, diagrams, and note cards in your presentation. Speak clearly and confidently as you make your speech.

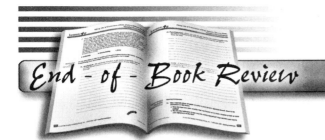
Multiple Choice
Read the following questions and the four possible answers. Choose the answer to each question. Find the bubble next to the question that has the same letter as the answer you chose. Fill in this bubble to mark your answer.

Ⓐ Ⓑ Ⓒ Ⓓ
1. **If a report or speech tries to convince an audience to accept an idea or suggestion, what is its purpose?**
  a. persuade   c. instruct
  b. entertain   d. give directions

Ⓐ Ⓑ Ⓒ Ⓓ
2. **Which of the following terms describes the author's opinion or feelings about a topic or subject?**
  a. closing   c. main idea
  b. opening   d. point of view

Ⓐ Ⓑ Ⓒ Ⓓ
3. **Which word describes making a written report or story available to others in print?**
  a. publish   c. speak in public
  b. present   d. edit

Ⓐ Ⓑ Ⓒ Ⓓ
4. **What type of literature is presented as plays?**
  a. nonfiction   c. poetry
  b. drama   d. word pictures

Ⓐ Ⓑ Ⓒ Ⓓ
5. **What literary device compares two things using the words "like" or "as"?**
  a. metaphor   c. simile
  b. foreshadowing   d. symbol

Ⓐ Ⓑ Ⓒ Ⓓ
6. **What literary device is used to give human qualities to nonhuman things?**
  a. foreshadowing   c. personification
  b. metaphor   d. simile

Ⓐ Ⓑ Ⓒ Ⓓ
7. **What are opinions?**
  a. a person's central ideas   c. a person's beliefs
  b. a person's topics   d. a person's ideas that can be proved

Ⓐ Ⓑ Ⓒ Ⓓ
8. **Which technique is the best one to use for organizing facts and ideas in order of importance?**
  a. finding a source   c. outlining
  b. finding a topic   d. plagiarizing

9. **What does it mean to paraphrase a piece of writing?**
  a. rewrite it in your own words   c. copy it word for word
  b. translate it into another language   d. analyze its meaning

Language Arts

10. **In the questioning procedure the *Five W's and the H*, what does H stand for?**
    a. how?
    c. home or away?
    b. he or she?
    d. how long ago?

11. **What is the topic of a story or article?**
    a. the main idea that the author or speaker wants to present
    b. the subject, or what the story or article tells about
    c. the details that give more information
    d. the background of the story or article

12. **What is the central idea of a story or article?**
    a. the main point the author or speaker wants to present about the topic
    b. the subject, or what the story or article tells about
    c. the author or speaker's point of view
    d. the middle part of the story or article

13. **Which of the following describes a poem written in meter?**
    a. It has the same number of words in each line.
    b. It has the same basic rhythm in each line.
    c. It has groups of lines that repeat.
    d. It has rhyming words at the end of each line.

14. **What does an author or speaker do when he or she makes an audience laugh, feel sad, or experience suspense?**
    a. inform
    c. persuade
    b. entertain
    d. instruct

15. **What is a stanza?**
    a. the rhythm of a poem
    c. a figure of speech in a poem
    b. groups of lines that repeat in a poem
    d. the theme of a poem

16. **What is the purpose of a campaign speech by a candidate for President?**
    a. inform
    c. persuade
    b. entertain
    d. instruct

17. **What do you look at when you use context clues to determine the meaning of an unfamiliar word?**
    a. the dictionary
    b. the end of the story
    c. the words and sentences around the unfamiliar word
    d. the words of a character in the story

End - of - Book Review

18. What is an opinion?

    a. what someone finds out about a topic from a reference book

    b. what someone infers from hints and clues

    c. what someone believes to be right or prefers

    d. what someone figures out from the details

19. What kind of graphic is used to organize simple lists of information?

    a. table

    b. circle graph

    c. bar graph

    d. line graph

20. What does a map legend provide?

    a. details about one particular place

    b. a main idea about the entire world

    c. a complete list of cities in the world

    d. a list of map symbols and what they represent

21. What do you call the person who controls the artistic elements in a film?

    a. director

    b. writer

    c. producer

    d. author

22. Which of the following can be shown on a map?

    a. the habitat of a certain animal

    b. the area where tornadoes are most likely to occur

    c. the locations of the largest cities in the U.S.

    d. all of the above

23. Which of the following is used most often nowadays to commemorate an important event?

    a. etching

    b. drawing

    c. photograph

    d. painting

24. Which kind of graphic shows how parts compare to a whole?

    a. table

    b. line graph

    c. bar graph

    d. circle graph

25. What does "adapt" mean?

    a. to create an original work

    b. to change from the original literary work

    c. to copy an existing work word for word

    d. to rename an original work

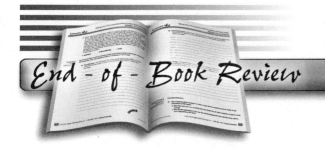

Writing Prompt ● The Greatest Act of Kindness

Situation

A newspaper editor has asked you to contribute a piece to the local paper. The theme is "What is the greatest act of kindness you've ever witnessed?" Write a brief selection answering this question.

Before You Write

As you prepare to write your entry, think about the following ideas:

● What purpose will you have in writing: entertain, inform, persuade, or instruct?

● What is your topic and central idea?

● What details do you want to include?

● What literary form will you use?

● What literary devices, such as simile, metaphor, symbolism, and irony, might be included?

● What conclusions do you want your readers to draw from your piece?

Write a paper answering the question above. Use any style of writing that you choose. As you write, be sure to think about your topic, main idea or theme, supporting details, opinions, and conclusions. Complete your work on a separate piece of paper. You may wish to write in your literary response journal instead.

Speaking Prompt ● A Biography of Yourself

Situation

For the television program "Great Biographies," you're preparing a biography of yourself. Tell your life story from birth to the present day.

Before You Speak

As you prepare your speech, think about the following ideas:

● What facts about yourself will be most interesting to the audience?

● What sources of information can you draw on, such as birth certificate, diaries, letters, grade cards, interviews with family members, etc.?

● How will you organize the events of your life, in chronological order or according to some other theme?

● How can you use graphic aids such as maps, charts, and tables?

● What pictures and photographs can you display?

● What conclusions do you want the audience to draw about your life?

Deliver a presentation about the story of your life. If possible, videotape the presentation and show it to several different groups. Be sure to include a topic, main idea or theme, supporting details, opinions, and conclusions. You can use such things as pictures, photographs, charts, diagrams, and note cards in your presentation. Speak clearly and confidently as you make your speech.

Writing Guidelines

As you write, be sure to:

1. Stick to your central idea or topic.
2. Include only those details, explanations, and examples that support your central idea.
3. Express your ideas in an order that is clear and that makes sense.
4. Clearly state your opening and closing.
5. Use varied sentence structure and word choice.
6. Link your opinions and conclusions directly to your central idea and topic.
7. Write neatly so that your work is easy to read.

Speaking Guidelines

As you speak, be sure to:

1. Stick to your central idea or topic.
2. Include only those details, explanations, and examples that support your central idea.
3. Express your ideas in an order that is clear and that makes sense.
4. Clearly state your opening and closing.
5. Use varied sentence structure and word choice.
6. Link your opinions and conclusions directly to your central idea and topic.
7. Speak loudly enough so that the audience can hear what you have to say.
8. Pace your speech so that it is not rushed, but don't speak so slowly that you lose the audience's interest.
9. Speak with emphasis to hold the audience's attention and to show you are interested in your topic.

Notes

Notes